MILLER FAMILY
COOKBOOK

. . . for you.

ISBN 0-9670704-2-2

Published by:

ABANA BOOKS
6523 TR 346 Millersburg, OH 44654

1

CANNING GUIDE

Pressure Canner
Let steam vent for 10 minutes to expel all air from the canner, then close the vent to let pressure build. Start timing after the pressure reaches 10 pounds. If pressure falls below 10 pounds at any time during processing, start the timing over again.

Vegetable	Time to maintain pressure for pints in minutes	Time to maintain pressure for quarts in minutes
Asparagus	25	30
Beets	30	35
Carrots	25	30
Corn	55	---
Cowpeas	35	40
Lima Beans	40	50
Potatoes	35	40
Pumpkin	55	90
Snap Beans	20	25
Winter Squash	55	90

Homecanned vegetables except tomatoes, should be cooked before they are served. Bring the vegetables to a rolling boil, then boil an additional 20 minutes for corn or spinach, 10 minutes for other vegetables.

Boiling Bath
Start to time only when the water reaches a rolling boil.

Fruit or Vegetable	Time in boiling water bath for pints in minutes		Time in boiling water baths for quarts in minutes	
	Hot pack	Raw pack	Hot pack	Raw pack
Apples	15	---	20	---
Apricots	20	25	25	30
Berries	10	10	15	15
Cherries	10	20	15	25
Peaches	20	25	25	30
Pears	20	25	25	30
Plums	20	20	25	25
Rhubarb	10	---	10	---
Sauerkraut	15	15	20	20
Tomatoes	35	40	45	50
Tomato juice	35	---	35	---

PURE HOMEGROWN SORGHUM
It is a fabulus natural sweetener

Extracting Sorghum Juice

WHAT IS SORGHUM
Sorghum is made from 100% percent pure, natural juice extracted from sorghum cane. The juice is cleansed of impurities and concentrated by evaporation in open pans into a clear, amber colored, mild flavored syrup. The syrup retains all of its natural sugars and other nutrients. It is 100 percent natural and contains NO chemical additives of any kind

Sorghum is one of the oldest natural sweeteners known. It was the "principal sweetener" used by our ancestors as America was being settled. The sorghum cooking pan traveled westward with the settlers. It, thus, became a part of America's heritage besides being the energy food of the settlers, sorghum made their foods more tasty and nutritious. Sorghum contains such hard to find nutrients as calcium, iron, potassium and phosphorous.

The settlers found many ways in using sorghum --sweetening drinks, making confections, flavoring meats --but its most popular usage was in baking. It was used in place of sugar in making pies, breads, puddings .and countless cakes and cookies.

The versatility of sorghum is being rediscovered by today's nutrition conscious homemakers. They are finding that there is hardly a food served today that sorghum will not improve. Sorghum blends with every kind of food, enhancing both taste and texture in very subtle ways. For today's chef, sorghum is a nutritious flavoring, a seasoning ingredient and a sugar substitute. It is that secret ingredient that gives any food that delicious taste and aroma that spells H-O-M-E-M-A-D-E. Try our suggested recipes-- but don't stop there. Be venturesome. Experiment with your own favorite dishes and discover the real goodness of sorghum.

Send your inquiries to:
Heritage Acres
10750 W 450 N
Shipshewana, IN 46565

3

MEASURES

3 teaspoons = 1 tablespoon
4 tablespoons = 1/4 cup
2 cups = 1 pint
1 lb. butter = 2 cups
1 lb. granulated sugar = 2 cups
1 lb. confectioner's sugar = 3 1/2 cups
1 lb. flour = 4 cups
1 square chocolate = 1 ounce
Butter the size of an egg = 1/4 cup
8-10 egg whites = 1 cup
12-14 egg yolks = 1 cup
1 tablespoon cornstarch = 2 tablespoons flour
1 1/2 tablespoons lemon juice plus sweet milk to make 1 cup sour milk
Wayne & Kathryn Miller

Table Blessings

We thank you God for happy hearts,
For rain and sunny weather.
We thank you God for this, our food,
And that we are together.

(Sung to the tune of Edelweiss)
Bless our friends,
Bless our food,
Come, O Lord, and sit with us.
May our speech,
Glow with peace,
And your love surround us.
Bless our friends,
Bless our food,
Come, O Lord, and be with us.

Lieber Gott ich bin klein
Mache du mine hertze rein
Lasz niemand drein wonnen als Jesus allein.

Speisz Gott, trank Gott, all die arme kinder
Die auf erden sind. Amen.

God is Great and God is Good,
And we thank Him for our food,
By His hands we all are fed,
Give us Lord, our daily bread. Amen

Gott dir sei dank fur diese gaben
Die wir jetz empfangen haben
Und bitten dich als unsern herrn
Uns dieses ferner zu beschern
Auch einstens mit dir, O Lieber Gott
In freut zu leben ewig dort. Amen.

Great God the giver of all good,
Accept our thanks and bless our food,
Grace, health and strength to us afford,
Through Jesus Christ, our loving Lord.

For Balmy sunshine,
For nourishing rain,
Dear Father in Heaven we thank Thee
Thy food and Thy care
Rich blessings we share
Proof of Thy goodness,
We thank Thee
We thank Thee , Oh God. Amen

We thank Thee for our daily bread
Let also, Lord, our souls be fed
Oh Bread of Life from day to day
Sustain us on our homeward way.

Feed Thy children, Father holy,
Comfort sinners meek and lowly.
May Thy blessings now be spoken,
O'er the bread before us broken.
That it serve us while we're living
Health and strenth to each one giving
Till at last with saints we're able
To surround thy heavenly table.

May all that we do and all that we say,
Help to brighten someone's day
And may this meal give strength today,
To do your will at work and at play.

BEVERAGES

Wm & Emma Miller Homestead Farmhouse

Miller Kitchen Centerpiece

Art work throughout this book is contributed by two of the "Miller girls," most of which was originally drawn for published greeting cards.

6

BUTTERMILK DRINK

1 egg   Ice cream
Buttermilk (store bought)
Beat the egg and add the buttermilk until glass is 3/4 full. Fill up the rest of the way with ice cream. You may add a sweetener to taste. We like to add Eagle brand milk. This drink is a real energizer.
Yield: 1 serving
Monroe & Elsie Miller

CITRUS SLUSH

2 1/2 c. sugar
3 c. water
1 - 12 oz. can frozen orange juice concentrate
1 - 12 oz. can frozen lemonade concentrate
1 - 12 oz. pineapple juice
3 c. cold water
4 qt. lemon-lime soda, chilled
In a 6 qt. kettle, bring sugar and water to a boil, stirring until sugar dissolves. Remove from heat. Stir in frozen lemonade and orange juice until melted. Stir in pineapple juice and cold water until well blended, pour into 2 - 9 X 13 pans. Cover and freeze overnight or until mixture is firm. Cut each pan into 24 squares. Place squares into a 2 gal. punch bowl or other container. Slowly pour chilled soda over squares. Stir until punch is slushy.
Yield: 32 - 1 c. servings
Glen & Sue Ellen Borkholder

COLD TEA

Take some fresh garden tea, as much as is desired. Put it in a large bowl and cover with cold water. Take some in each hand and rub together, bruising the leaves and stems well. Repeat, as desired, for more flavor. Let stand up to an hour. Strain, sweeten to taste, and chill before serving.
Urie & Lizzie Ann Miller

EGG NOG

1 egg, well beaten   1 c. chilled rich milk
2 T. sugar   Vanilla (optional)
          Beat together well and serve.

Blessed are the flexible. For they shall not be bent out of shape!

FRUIT POPS

1 c. bananas (about 2 med.)
10 oz. frozen berries (any kind you like)
1 3/4 c. crushed pineapple with juice
2/3 c. evaporated milk
Put all together in blender and mix well. Pour into 5 oz. paper cups and place a stick in each cup and freeze.

FRUIT SLUSH

2 c. sugar
3 c. water
1 - 6 oz. can frozen orange juice concentrate, diluted
8 ripe bananas
1 - #2 can crushed pineapple with juice
Mix sugar and water; boil for five minutes and let cool. Add the rest of the ingredients to the syrup. Slice or crush the bananas and stir. Freeze. Thaw to a light slush and serve. Bananas will not darken. Peaches, pears, and grapes may be added for different flavor.
Jacob & Loretta Shetler   Barbara Miller

HOT CHOCOLATE DRINK MIX

8 c. dry milk (Carnation is best)
1 c. dry coffee cream
1 c. sugar (may be powdered)
1 lb. can Nestles instant cocoa
Mix thoroughly. Add 1/4 c. mixture to one c. of boiling water. It's delicious. Enjoy!

HOT SPICY CIDER

1 c. orange juice
1 tsp. allspice
1 tsp. cloves
3 cinnamon sticks
1 T. lemon juice
1 gal. cider
Sugar to taste
Simmer the above ingredients for 6-8 minutes. Drink hot.
Yield: 16 servings
Monroe & Elsie Miller

HOT VANILLA MILK

Add 1" of vanilla bean and 1 tsp. honey to a glass of milk and bring to a near boil. You may add a pinch of cinnamon or other pure spice. You may even use vanilla extract.

LABOR ADE

1/3 c. ReaLemon   1/2 tsp. baking soda
1/3 c. honey   6 c. warm water
1 tsp. salt
Whenever you drink this, pour a cup, add 2-3 crushed calcium tabs
and stir briskly. Drink leisurely. Calcium helps ease pains.

LEMONADE

1 c. fresh lemon juice   1 1/2 qt. water
1 c. honey
Bring honey and water to a boil if you plan to keep it several days.
Then add lemon juice and store in the refrigerator.

MAPLE MILK SHAKE

For each milk shake, blend or shake together: 1 glass of milk and 2
T. maple syrup. Remember, all milk gets boiled.

PINEAPPLE JUICE

Peel a pineapple.   Remove all soft spots.   Cut it into cubes.
Extract the juice by putting the pineapple through a food grinder or
a blender. There will be very little pulp. Strain the juice and serve
it on ice with sprigs of mint. Makes about 1 1/2 cups of juice. Mix
the pulp with an equal amount of clover honey and use as topping
(kept in freezer) for homemade ice cream, pancakes, or yogurt.

POPSICLES

1 pkg. Jello   2 c. hot water
1 pkg. Kool-Aid   4 c. cold water
2/3 c. sugar
Dissolve Jello, Kool-Aid, and sugar in hot water.   Add the cold
water and freeze in ice cube trays. After adding ingredients to ice
cube tray, place a piece of Saran Wrap over top of tray and place
toothpicks into Kool-Aid for sticks.

QUICK ROOT BEER

2 c. white sugar   3 or 4 tsp. root beer extract
3/4 or 1 tsp. yeast
Dissolve yeast in warm water for 15 min. Dissolve sugar in 3 1/2
qt. water and extract while yeast sets. Mix together in 1 gal. jug.
Cap. Let set in warm place for 1 day. Refrigerate or cool.
DeLilah Stoll

RHUBARB JUICE

2 qt. rhubarb juice
2 1/4 c. sugar
2 T. Jello (strawberry or raspberry)
1 pkg. Kool-Aid (strawberry, raspberry or tropical punch)
1 c. unsweetened pineapple juice
1/3 c. Real Lemon
2 c. hot water or 1 c. water and 1 c. rhubarb juice
Cut the rhubarb in big chunks. Fill a kettle half full then put in water to 3/4 full. j Cook until mushy then drain well. Mix all together then put in jars and cold pack 20 minutes. When serving, dilute with water or lemon-lime soda.
Ivan & Martha Miller

RHUBARB DRINK

4 qt. rhubarb juice
1 can frozen orange juice
1 can frozen lemonade

7 qt. water
2 pkg. raspberry Kool-Aid
4 c. sugar

In an 8-qt. kettle, put half full of chopped rhubarb and fill with water; bring to a boil and let stand 30 minutes. Drain. Add rest of the ingredients. This can be canned.
Paul & Rhonda Borkholder

SODA POP

Put 1 tsp. citric acid, 2 T. vegetable glycerin, 2 T. honey, and 1 lemon, juiced by hand, into a quart jar and fill with cold water. Refrigerate until ready to use. Then add 1 tsp. baking soda (chemically pure only) and shake a few times, keeping the lid tight. Pour over a few ice cubes. Excellent for stomach distress. Many variations are possible: other fruit concentrates, made in the blender, can be used along with some lemon juice; for example, 2 blended whole apples (peeled), blended pineapple, orange or grapefruit. Always add a bit of lemon to give it zip. You may add a pinch of ginger or other spice.
NOTE: The amount of sodium in 1/2 tsp. baking soda is .476 grams. If you have heart disease, high blood pressure, or edema, use potassium bicarbonate instead. Ask your doctor what an acceptable amount of sodium or potassium bicarbonate is. I would suggest limiting yourself to one glass of soda pop a day, even if you do not have heart disease. The citric acid kills bacteria, while the carbonation brings relief.

The soul would have no rainbows if the eyes had no tears.

TOMATO JUICE

12 medium tomatoes
1/2 c. water
1 slice onion

2 ribs celery with leaves
1/2 bay leaf and
3 sprigs parsley

Strain these ingredients. Simmer for 1/2 hr. Season with:
1 tsp. salt (aluminum free)
1/2 tsp. honey

1/4 tsp. paprika

Serve thoroughly chilled.
Yield: About 4 servings.

YANKEE DRINK

1 gal. water
3 c. honey
1 tsp. ginger
1/2 c. fresh lemon juice or distilled white vinegar
Mix together and serve.

BREAD I

In a large bowl, mix a stiff dough of:

1/2 c. sugar
1/2 c. corn oil
1 T. salt

1 1/2 c. starter
1 1/2 c. warm water (not hot)
6 c. plain flour

Place dough in greased bowl, grease dough and turn it over. Cover with plastic wrap and let rise overnight (8-12 hours) at room temperature. (Make this bread in the evening and let rise all night.) Next morning, punch down and divide into three parts. Knead each part 8-10 times on a well-floured board. Place bread in greased loaf pans and brush tops with oil. Cover with plastic wrap and let rise 4-5 hours (all day is fine). Bake on bottom rack of oven at 350º for 30-35 minutes. Remove and brush with melted butter. Allow to cool on rack. Wrap bread well to keep from drying out. Bread may be frozen or reheated.
Sam & Ruby Miller

BREAD II

3 c. warm water
1 T. salt
1T. sugar

3 T. yeast
4 c. flour, white or wheat

Mix above ingredients and let stand until "bubbly", then add:

1/2 c. sugar dissolved in
1 c. warm water

1 c. oil
Blend well

Now add flour, only 2 c. at a time. Mix well after each addition. It takes about 10 c. flour or until it feels smooth and elastic. Let rise until double in size. Then work out in 4 bread pans. Let rise and bake at 350º for 25-30 min. For cinnamon bread, roll out with rolling pin and put butter, white sugar and cinnamon on dough. Roll up tight and place seam-side down in pan and sprinkle cinnamon and sugar on top. Bake the same as you would any other bread.
Linda (Willis) Bontrager

When teaching a child to tie his shoes, make the first tie, then make a loop saying, "This is a tree." Then take the other string around the loop saying, "This is a rabbit running around the tree." And while pushing the string through to make the next loop say, "This is the hole where the rabbit runs in." When the tie is made, hold up the two loops and say, "Here are his two ears."

BREAD III

1/4 c. brown sugar	2 c. hot water
1/4 c. white sugar	6 tsp. yeast
1/4 c. oil	2 tsp. sugar
1/4 c. honey	1 c. warm water
1/4 c. shortening, melted	2 c. whole wheat flour
3 tsp. salt	6-7 c. white flour

Note: White flour can be used instead of whole wheat. Mix sugars, honey, oil, shortening, salt and hot water. Let cool to lukewarm. Mix yeast, sugar and warm water, let rise until foamy. Mix yeast and shortening mixtures together and add flour. Let rise 1 hour, punch down. Let rise 1 more hour. Put in pans. Let rise 1 1/2 hours. Bake at 325º for approximately 22 minutes.
Yield: 4 loaves
Paul & Rhonda Borkholder

GOOD HOMEMADE BREAD

1 c. lukewarm water	1 tsp. sugar
2 pkg. yeast or 2 level T.	

Mix above ingredients and let set five minutes. Add:

1/3 c. wesson oil	6 c. bread flour
1/2 c. sugar or 1/3 c. honey	Add and beat well:
2 tsp. salt	Yeast mix
2 c. hot water	Add:
Add and beat well:	3 c. additional flour

Punch dough down three times. Put dough in bread pans (four if pans are small or three if pans are big). Bake 300º to 350º for 30-45 minutes. Put in bags after cool. For brown bread add 2 c. wheat flour and 2 c. less white.
Yield: 3-4 loaves
Alva & Katie Ann Bontrager

OATMEAL BREAD

9 tsp. salt	4 c. oatmeal
3/4 c. honey	4 c. cold water
1/4 c. brown sugar	3 T. instant yeast
1/2 c. vegetable oil	10-12 c. bread flour
1/2 c. lard	

Pour four c. hot water over the first 6 ingredients and let set for 15 minutes. Add the cold water, instant yeast and bread flour to stiffen. Let rise until double in size. Work out.
Yield: 8 loaves

A gossiper is like an old shoe; it's tongue never stays in place.

GOOD WHITE BREAD
In a small bowl, take 1 c. lukewarm water and mix 1 T. sugar in it, add 2 T. yeast and let set. In a large bowl, take 1/2 c. sugar and 1 T. salt, 1/2 c. Wesson oil and 1 qt. warm water. Mix together and add 2 c. flour and beat. After yeast has risen, add to flour mixture and add 2 more c. of flour, beating hard (with wooden spoon or large spoon with holes) until very fluffy. Keep on adding flour 1-2 c. at a time and beating hard after each addition, when dough gets too stiff to beat, using your hands and work in enough flour to make a soft dough, greasing hands occasionally. Grease top of dough lightly and cover with a clean cloth. Let rise in a warm place for 30 minutes, then knead down and repeat 2 times at one hour intervals. Form into loaves and stick each loaf with a fork several times to prevent large air bubbles. When doubled in size and loaf feels light in weight, start baking in 275º oven for 20 minutes. Increase heat to 375º and bake until browned, about one hour.
Yield: 4 lg. loaves
Wayne & Kathryn Miller

SOUR DOUGH BREAD
Starter: Put initial starter in refrigerator 3-5 days. Then take it out and feed it with the following:

1/2 c. sugar	1 c. plain flour
3 T. instant potatoes	1 c. warm (not hot) water

Mix this well and stir into starter in glass bowl. Let stand out of the refrigerator all day (8-12 hours). This will not rise, only bubble. Take out 1 1/2 cup starter to use in bread and return remaining starter to refrigerator. Keep in refrigerator 3-5 days, then feed it again. if you do not make bread, throw out 1 cup of starter, but continue to feed remaining starter every 3-5 days.
Sam & Ruby Miller

BROWN BREAD

4 1/2 c. warm water	4 T. yeast
3/4 c. honey or molasses	

Let set until foamy. Add:
1 1/4 c. oil
2 eggs, beaten
5 tsp. salt
3 c. oatmeal
6 c. brown flour (We like spelt flour)
Beat well and let rise until double in size, then finish with Gigantic Action Bread Flour.
Joni & Emma Sue Miller

WHOLE WHEAT OATMEAL BREAD

2 1/2 c. boiling water
1 T. salt
1/4 c. cooking oil
1 c. lukewarm water
Whole wheat flour

2 c. quick oats
1 c. honey
4 eggs, beaten
2 T. yeast

Pour boiling water over oatmeal and set aside to cool to a lukewarm temperature. Dissolve yeast in lukewarm water. Beat the remaining ingredients together, making sure batter is warm, not hot, before adding yeast. Work in enough flour to make a nice spongy type dough that is not sticky. Place in greased bowl and grease the top of the dough, then cover and let rise in a warm place until doubled in size, about 35-40 minutes. Punch down and let rise again. Shape into six loaves and let rise. Bake at 350º for 30 minutes or until golden brown. Brush the top with butter and cool.
Monroe & Elsie Miller

BANANA NUT BREAD

1/2 c. butter
1 c. sugar
2 eggs, beaten together
1 c. over-ripe bananas

2 c. flour
1 tsp. soda
1/2 tsp. salt
1/2 c. nuts, optional

Mix the butter, sugar and eggs together. Mash the bananas and add to the mixture. Mix the remaining ingredients and pour batter into greased bread pan. Bake at 350º for 60-65 minutes. Remove from pan when cool. Good with butter or jelly.
Alva & Katie Ann Bontrager

DILLY CASSEROLE BREAD

1 pkg. yeast
1/4 c. warm water
1 c. cottage cheese
2 T. sugar
1 T. onion, minced
1 T. butter
2 tsp. dill seed
1 tsp. salt
1/4 tsp. baking soda
1 egg

Mix all ingredients together and add 2 to 2 1/2 c. flour to form a stiff dough. Let rise until doubled in size. Stir down and let rise again. Put in pans until doubled in size again. Bake at 350º for 40-50 minutes.
Herman & Carolina Miller

CAN-DO-QUICK SWEET DOUGH

2 pkg. yeast
1/2 c. warm water
1 1/4 c. buttermilk
2 eggs
5 1/2 c. flour

1 c. butter
1/2 c. sugar
2 tsp. baking powder
2 tsp. salt

Drop by spoonful in pan. Make a small dent with finger. Fill with pie filling and let rise. Glaze after done baking.
Jacob & Loretta Shetler

LINDA'S PANCAKES

2 beaten eggs
2 c. sour milk
1 tsp. baking soda
2 tsp. baking powder

1 1/2 tsp. salt
1/4 c. oil
2 1/4 c. flour

Mix in the order given. I put a little butter on my square skillet when I start frying them, but don't use anything after that. They don't taste as greasy that way. I cook about 3 c. diced potatoes, some onion and a can of beef chunks (salt and pepper) together. Add some water, then thicken with milk and flour so it's like gravy. Very good on pancakes.
Linda (Willis) Bontrager

SWEET MILK PANCAKES

2 c. flour
4 tsp. baking powder
2 T. sugar
1/2 tsp. salt

1 3/4 c. milk
2 eggs, beaten
2 T. butter melted

Mix dry ingredients. Add milk, butter and eggs. Bake on griddle over medium heat.
Yield: 18 cakes
Joni & Emma Sue Miller   David & Mary Kauffman

MY FAVORITE PANCAKES

2 1/4 c. flour (may use part whole wheat)
4 T. baking powder
2 T. sugar

1 tsp. baking soda
2 eggs
2 c. buttermilk
1/4 c. salad oil

Sift dry ingredients together; set aside. Combine eggs, buttermilk and salad oil. Add dry ingredients, stirring until flour is just moistened (batter will be lumpy). Pour on hot oiled griddle. Turn over once. I use milk and vinegar instead of buttermilk.
Mabel (DeVon) Miller

SOUR DOUGH PANCAKES

Feed starter the night before.
1/2 c. sugar
3 T. instant potatoes
1 c. plain flour
1 c. warm (not hot) water
Take 2 cups of starter, put rest back in refrigerator.
Add:

1 egg   1 T. sugar
1 tsp. baking soda   2 T. oil

Makes approximately 18 - 4" pancakes. Pancakes are light and fluffy. Use caution when flipping, pancakes are soft.
Sam & Ruby Miller

OATMEAL PANCAKES

2 c. cornmeal   1 T. baking soda
2 c. whole wheat flour   1 T. salt
2 c. quick oats   3 eggs, separated
1 T. baking powder   1/2 c. cooking oil
1 1/2 qt. sweet milk, approx.

Mix the dry ingredients thoroughly. Add egg yolks, oil and milk that has been warmed to lukewarm and mix well. Fold in beaten egg whites. Bake on a greased griddle, turning once.
Yield: 45-50 pancakes
Urie & Lizzie Ann Miller

FOUNDATION SWEET ROLLS

1 c. milk, scalded   1/2 tsp. nutmeg
1/2 c. sugar   1 T. sugar
1 1/2 tsp. salt   2 T. instant yeast
1/2 c. Wesson oil   1 c. lukewarm water
2 eggs, beaten   7 c. sifted bread flour

Pour scalded milk over sugar, salt and oil - add eggs, and beat well. Dissolve yeast in lukewarm water. Add yeast to the rest of the ingredients. Add flour gradually, beating well. Knead lightly working in just enough flour so that dough can be handled. Place dough in greased bowl and cover and let rise one hour (double size). Roll and cut in 1 thick slices. Let rise until light, about 1 hour. Bake in moderate oven. Frost with powdered sugar frosting.
Wayne & Kathryn Miller

Oh Lord, bless the person who is too busy to worry in the daytime and too sleepy to worry at night.

CINNAMON ROLLS

2 c. sugar
1 1/2 c. shortening
4 tsp. salt

4 eggs, beaten
4 T. yeast
5 c. warm water

Dissolve yeast in water. Combine sugar, shortening, salt and eggs. Add water and yeast; mix well. Beat in flour. Let rise until double in size. Roll out. Spread on butter, brown sugar and a little cinnamon. Put on pans; let rise 45-60 minutes. Bake at 425º.
Yield: 4 doz.
Glen & Sue Ellen Borkholder

DONUTS OR ROLLS

2 sticks butter
2 c. milk (scalded)
2/3 c. sugar
4 tsp. salt
2 c. lukewarm water

3 pkg. active dry yeast
12 c. bread flour
6 eggs, beaten
Vanilla

Scald milk - combine scalded milk, butter, sugar, and salt. Let set until butter melts. Add cold water. Mix yeast into 1/2 c. lukewarm water. Add to mixture. Add six c. flour. Add beaten eggs and beat thoroughly. Add remaining flour until all mixed in never adding more or less. Let rise to double in size, then stir down. Roll out and spread with melted butter, cinnamon, and sugar. Roll up and cut. Let rise and then bake at 375(for 15-20 minutes. These are really good with caramel icing. I also use this for coffee cakes and spread with frosting and fruit filling like cherry or strawberry.
Yield: 4 doz.
Linda (Willis) Bontrager

ELLEN'S CARROT MUFFINS

3 c. flour
1 tsp. baking soda
1 1/2 T. baking powder
1/2 tsp. salt
1 tsp. cinnamon
2 c. bran
4 eggs

1 tsp. vanilla
1 1/2 c. vegetable oil
1 1/4 c. dark brown sugar
1/4 c. molasses
3 c. finely grated carrots
1 c. raisins

Mix together first 5 ingredients with wire whip, add bran and mix. Beat eggs and add oil, sugar and molasses. Add carrots and raisins. I put cupcake liners in muffin tins. Bake at 350º for 25 minutes. A moist muffin that's a favorite in lunches.
Yield: 24 muffins
Ellen W. Bontrager

CORNBREAD

3 c. cornmeal
2 c. flour
6 tsp. baking powder
1/2 c. shortening
Bake till done.
Monroe W. Miller

1 c. sugar
3 eggs
2 1/2 c. milk

LEMON MUFFINS

1/2 c. butter, softened
1/2 c. sugar
2 eggs, separated
1 c. all purpose flour
1 tsp. Baking powder

1/4 tsp. Salt
3 T. lemon juice
1 T. grated lemon peel
Cinnamon

Cream butter and sugar. Add the egg yolks and mix well. Combine flour, baking powder and salt; add alternately with lemon juice to creamed mixture. Beat egg whites until stiff peaks form; fold into batter with lemon peel. Fill greased or paper lined muffin cups 2/3 full. Sprinkle with cinnamon. Bake at 350º for 20-25 minutes or until light golden brown and a toothpick inserted in the center comes out clean.
Yield: 9 muffins

BISCUITS SUPREME

2 c. flour
1/2 tsp. salt
2 tsp. sugar
1/2 c. shortening

4 tsp. baking powder
1/2 tsp. cream of tartar
2/3 c. milk

Sift dry ingredients together. Cut in shortening until mixture resembles coarse crumbs. Add milk all at once and stir just until dough follows fork around bowl. Roll 1/2 thick. Cut with biscuit cutter. Place on a greased cookie sheet and bake at 350º until golden brown.
Mary J. Miller (Joni)

BISCUITS

2 c. flour
3 tsp. baking powder
1 tsp. salt

1/2 c. oil
3/4 c. sour milk

Blend first 3 ingredients, then pour the liquid in together and mix all at once. This is enough for 1 pan of biscuits. I also use this recipe for pizza dough and apple dumplings, etc., adding a bit more flour and also some to roll out dough.
Linda (Willis) Bontrager

FAMILY REUNION BUNS

2/3 c. sugar
2/3 c. milk
1 tsp. salt
1/3 c. butter

2/3 c. warm water
2 T. dry yeast
3 eggs, beaten
6 3/4 c. flour

Scald milk and cool to lukewarm. Add sugar, salt and melted butter. Add yeast and warm water until yeast dissolves. Add beaten egg and work in the flour. Let the dough rise until double in bulk, about one hour. Then divide dough in half. Cut each half into 12 equal parts and form into balls. Place two inches apart on a greased cookie sheet. Brush with butter and let rise, about one hour. Bake at 400º for 20 minutes.
Yield: 24 buns
Monroe & Elsie Miller

DINNER ROLLS

2 c. self-rising flour
1 c. sweet milk

1/2 c. salad dressing
1 tsp. sugar

Preheat oven to 450º. Work up with a spoon into a soft ball. Bake for 10 minutes.
Yield: 1 doz.

LUNCHEON PAN ROLLS

1 c. scalded milk
2 T. butter
1/4 c. sugar

1 tsp. salt
2 eggs
4 c. bread flour

1 pkg. yeast, dissolved in 1/4 c. warm water
Scald milk. Add butter, sugar, salt and let stand till lukewarm. When lukewarm, add eggs, yeast, 1 1/2 c. flour. Beat for two minutes. Beat one minute longer while adding 1/2 c. flour. Stir in rest of flour with spoon. Let dough rise until double in size. Place on floured board and knead one minute. Shape, place on pan. Let rise until double in size again. Bake for 15-20 minutes at 425º.
Yield: 20 dinner rolls

ZUCCHINI BREAD

3 c. flour
1 1/2 c. white sugar
3 eggs, beaten
1 c. oil
1 tsp. Cinnamon

1 tsp. Salt
3/4 tsp. Soda
2 c. zucchini, unpeeled
2 c. nuts
1 c. raisins

Mix well and pour into loaf pans. Bake at 325º for 1 hour.
Yield: 2 loaves

MORMON MUFFINS

2 c. boiling water
5 tsp. Baking soda
1 c. shortening
2 c. sugar
4 eggs
5 c. all purpose flour

1 tsp. Salt
1 qt. Buttermilk
4 c. All-Bran
2 c. Bran Flakes
1 c. chopped walnuts

Combine water and baking soda; stir until dissolved and cool. Cream shortening and sugar. Add eggs one at a time, beating well after each addition. Combine flour and salt; add to creamed mixture alternately with buttermilk. Mix well and beat in the water mixture. Fold in the cereals and nuts. Fill greased or paper lined muffin cups 3/4 full. Bake at 350º for 25-30 minutes or until muffins test is done. This batter will keep in the refrigerator for 1 week and longer in the freezer.
Yield: 5 doz.

ICEBOX BUTTERHORNS

1 pkg. (1/4 oz.) active dry yeast
2 T. warm water (110º-115º)
2 c. warm milk (110º-115º)
1/2 c. sugar
1 egg, beaten
1 tsp. salt
6 c. all-purpose flour
3/4 c. butter or margarine, melted
Additional melted butter

In a large bowl, dissolve yeast in water. Add milk, sugar, egg, salt and three c. flour; beat until smooth. Beat in butter and remaining flour (dough will be sticky). Place in a greased bowl. Cover and refrigerate overnight. Punch dough down and divide in half. On a floured surface, roll each half into a 12 inch circle. Cut each circle into 12 pie-shaped wedges. Beginning at the wide end, roll up each wedge. Place rolls, point down, two inches apart on greased baking sheets. Cover and let rise for one hour. Bake at 350º for 15-20 minutes. Brush with melted butter.
Yield: 2 doz.
Neal & Emma Yoder

BREAKFAST BURRITOS

12 eggs
1 bag frozen hash browns
1 lg. onion, chopped
1 green pepper, chopped
1/2 lb. bulk pork sausage, bacon or ham browned and drained
12 flour tortillas, 10" (warmed)
3 c. (12 oz.) shredded cheddar cheese
Salsa (optional)
In large skillet, fry hash browns until browned; remove and set aside for a lg. bowl. Beat eggs, add onion and green pepper. Pour into the same skillet, cook and stir until eggs are set. Remove from heat. Add has browns and sausage, mix gently. Place about 3/4 c. of filling on each tortilla and top with about 1/4 c. of cheese. Roll up and place on a greased baking sheet. Bake at 350º for 15-20 min. or until heated through. Serve with salsa or sour cream.
Yield: 12 servings
Mabel (DeVon) Miller

BREAKFAST CEREAL

1 box (35 oz.) Cornflakes
20 c. quick oatmeal
1 pkg. sugar-coated puffed wheat (20 oz.)
Melt together:
1 c. brown sugar, packed
2 sticks butter
1 tsp. vanilla
1 tsp. maple flavoring
Pour the sugar mixture over the dry cereal. Dry in warm oven. Store in tight container. Serve with milk.
Ella E. Miller

BUMPERNICKEL

1 c. sour milk   2 tsp. baking soda
Thicken with graham flour (like cake batter)
Bake in a 9 X 13 pan at 350º for 30 min.
We often had this for breakfast. We'd cut cake in squares and steam on top of double boiler until warm, then we'd eat it with honey, milk and the huckleberries we used to can out of our own huckleberry mash - sometimes this was the only fruit we'd have to eat. I can still taste them!
Linda (Willis) Bontrager

CHEESE SOUFFLE

8 slices bread   1 T. onion salt
1 lb. cheese - Velveeta type   Salt
6 eggs, beaten   Pepper
2 c. milk
Cubed ham, smoky links, bacon, sausage, or mushrooms
Cube bread, put in bottom of casserole. Put cubed meat on top of bread. Slice cheese and put on top of meat. Mix eggs, milk and seasonings together and pour over top of the other ingredients. Refrigerate overnight. Bake at 325º for 45 minutes. Three batches is just right for a 10x15x3 cake pan, but needs to bake longer, at least one hour.
Raymond & Martha Bontrager

CORNMEAL MUSH

3 c. boiling water   1 c. cold water
1 tsp. salt   1 c. cornmeal
Mix cold water and cornmeal together and add to the 3 c. boiling water. Stir with a wire whisk right away, add salt. Stir until it starts boiling, then put the burner at the lowest and let it cook for 30 minutes. No need to stir. Eat it like that with butter and milk, or put it in a container, let cool, then refrigerate until cold. Slice and fry in butter until crisp.
Glen & Sue Ellen Borkholder

SAUSAGE GRAVY

1 lb. sage flavored sausage
2 T. finely chopped onion
6 T. flour
1 qt. Milk
1/2 tsp. Poultry seasoning
1/2 tsp. Ground nutmeg
1/4 tsp. Salt
Dash of Worcestershire sauce
Dash hot pepper sauce
Crumble sausage into a large saucepan; cook over medium low heat. Add onion; cook and stir until transparent. Drain, discarding all but 2 T of drippings. Stir in flour; cook over medium-low heat about 6 minutes or until mixture bubbles and turns golden. Stir in milk. Add seasonings; cook stirring until thickened.
Yield: 4-6 servings   (See section for biscuits)

Controlling other people's lives Is not a godly leader's trait
But serving other people's needs Is what the Lord considers great!

GRAPE NUTS I

6 1/2 c. brown sugar
2 c. buttermilk
1 1/4 tsp. salt
1/2 lb. butter
14 c. graham flour
3 tsp. baking soda
1 tsp. baking powder
2 T. vanilla
1 tsp. maple flavor
Bake at 350º until done. When cooled, crumble it and toast it.
Wayne & Kathryn Miller

GRAPE NUTS II

2 c. buttermilk
2 tsp. baking soda
2 tsp. salt

2 tsp. vanilla flavor
2 tsp. maple flavor

Stir together well, then add:

1/2 c. vegetable oil
2 c. brown sugar
2 c. bran

2 c. white flour
2 c. whole wheat flour

Mix sour milk, cream, vegetable oil, baking soda, salt, vanilla and maple flavors. Stir well, add sugar or molasses and stir in bran. Then add the flours. Let set overnight, bake next day. Soaks through and bakes better. Bake 300º - 350º. HINT: If edges are hard, then store overnight in tight container while warm. Edges will be soft to put through screen.
Yield: 2 cake pans
Delilah Stoll

EASY GRANOLA

18 c. oatmeal
4 c. coconut
2 c. brown sugar
2 c. wheat germ
2 c. nuts
2 c. raisins
1 c. sesame seeds

1 c. sunflower seeds
2/3 c. water
1 c. honey
1 c. butter
1 c. vegetable oil
2 tsp. vanilla
1 tsp. salt

Mix the dry ingredients together well. Heat the liquids until melted and then pour over oat mixture. Stir until well coated. Put a thin layer on cookie sheet and Toast at 350º for 15 minutes then turn oven down to 275º until golden. Stir occasionally.
Yield:
Joni & Emma Sue Miller   David & Mary Kauffman

26

LAURA'S GRANOLA

3 c. oil - mix to dry ingredients
28 c. oatmeal - regular
2 c. coconut
2 c. chopped pecans

2 c. sliced almonds
8 c. winter wheat bran
2 c. sunflower seeds

Mix the following and add to the oil and dry ingredients:

4 c. honey
1 c. water

2 T. salt
8 T. vanilla

Toast in pans at 250º for two hours, stirring every 15 minutes.
Yield: 45 c.
Oba & Laura Borkholder

NEW HORIZONS GRANOLA

5 c. oatmeal, uncooked (toasted 15-20 minutes)
1 c. apples, peeled and chopped
1 c. nuts, chopped
1 c. raisins
1 c. coconut

3/4 c. butter, melted
3/4 c. brown sugar
1 1/2 tsp. cinnamon

Bake 30-40 minutes, stirring occasionally to brown evenly.   Put the raisins in the last five minutes.
Yield: 9 c.
Jacob & Loretta Shetler

BAKED OATMELA

3 c. quick oatmeal
1 c. brown sugar
2 tsp. baking powder
1 1/2 tsp. cinnamon

1 tsp. salt
1 c. milk
2 eggs, beaten
1/2 c. butter, melted

Mix all ingredients together. Spoon into 9 baking dish. Bake at 350º for 40-45 minutes. Serve either warm or cold. A delicious breakfast cereal.
Yield:
Virgil & Esther Yoder

CAKES & FROSTINGS

Happy Birthday

AMERICAN BEAUTY RED CAKE

2 oz. red food coloring
3 T. instant cocoa
1/2 c. shortening (no liquid)
1 1/2 c. sugar
2 eggs
1 c. buttermilk
1/2 tsp. salt
2 1/2 c. flour
1 tsp. vanilla
1 T. vinegar
1 tsp. baking soda

Mix food coloring with cocoa and let stand. Cream shortening with sugar, add eggs and color mixture. Beat very well; add buttermilk, flour, salt and vanilla. Beat again. Add vinegar and soda. Pour into two greased paper-lined round 9 pans. Bake at 350º from 30-35 minutes. Cut each layer with thread while warm.
Yield:
Oba & Laura Borkholder

AMERICAN BEAUTY RED CAKE FROSTING

4 tsp. flour
1 c. milk
Pinch of salt
1 c. white sugar
1/2 c. butter
1/2 c. white shortening
1 T. vanilla

Mix the first three ingredients and cook until thick and smooth, stirring while cooking. Let cool. Mix the remaining ingredients and combine with the flour mixture, beat until fluffy. Ice between layers and on top, but not the sides. Never substitute butter for shortening.
Yield:
Oba & Laura Borkholder

ANGEL FOOD CAKE

2 c. egg whites
2 tsp. cream of tartar
1 c. white sugar
1 tsp. salt
1 1/3 c. Robin Hood flour
2/3 c. sugar (mixed with flour)
1 tsp. vanilla
1/2 tsp. almond extract

Beat the eggs, cream of tarter and salt together well until stiff peaks form. Add the 1 c. sugar slowly also beating it stiff. Sift the flour and the rest of the sugar together and add to the mixture of egg whites with wire whisk and flavor with 2 T. Jello or Kool-Aid and flavoring oil. Bake at 350º for 50 minutes and let it cool before you take it out of the pan.
Sam & Ruby Miller   Wayne & Kathryn Miller   Delilah Stoll

APPLE CAKE

2 c. flour
1 3/4 c. sugar
2/3 c. vegetable oil
1/3 c. water

1 tsp. baking soda
Dash of salt
1 egg
3 c. chopped apples

Mix the sugar, oil, water and egg - add the dry ingredients, then the apples. Bake in 350º oven.

Ivan & Martha Miller

APPLE DAPPLE CAKE

2 eggs, beaten
2 tsp. vanilla
2 c. sugar
1 c. Wesson oil

1/2 tsp. salt
3 c. flour
1 tsp. baking soda
4 c. shredded apples

Icing:

1 c. brown sugar
1/4 c. margarine

1/4 c. milk

Mix the eggs, vanilla, sugar and Wesson oil together. Sift the salt, flour and baking soda together and then add to the egg mixture along with the apples. Bake at 350º for 45 minutes or until done. It's best in a shallow cake sheet pan. For the icing, boil all the ingredients together for 2 1/2 minutes. Stir a little after removed from the heat but don't beat it. Add nuts, if desired. Drizzle over the cake while the cake and icing are still hot.

Yield:

Mabel (DeVon) Miller

APPLE DUMPLINGS

2 c. flour
1 tsp. salt
3 tsp. baking powder
1/3 c. oil

3/4 c. milk, sour
5 apples, peeled and cut in half

Sauce:

2 c. brown sugar
2 c. water

1/4 c. butter
1/2 tsp. cinnamon

Heat the above sauce ingredients in a saucepan.

Mix the dough ingredients and roll out and cut in about 8 or 10 squares (depends on how thin you roll it out). Place apple half on dough and put a spoonful of sugar in the center. Pull dough up and overlap to seal. Place in baking pan (round sides up). Then pour sauce over top and bake until browned and apples are tender. About 30 min. at 350º. I like to use yellow delicious apples for this.

Linda (Willis) Bontrager

APPLESAUCE CAKE

1/2 c. shortening
2 c. sugar
2 eggs
1 1/2 c. applesauce
2 1/2 c. sifted flour
1 1/2 tsp. baking soda
1 1/2 tsp. salt

1 tsp. cinnamon
1/2 tsp. cloves
1/2 tsp. allspice
1/2 c. water
1/2 c. nuts
1 c. raisins

Most cooks throw stuff together in their own fashion, and it comes out okay.
Sam & Ruby Miller

BAKE ON CAKE ICING

10 T. brown sugar
5 T. cream
1 tsp. vanilla

6 T. melted butter
1/2 c. coconut
1/2 c. nuts

Spread on hot cake and return to oven until it bubbles. Take out and cool.
Delilah Stoll

BETTER CAKE MIXES

3/4 c. flour
1/2 c. sugar
1 tsp. baking powder
1 T. vegetable oil

1/3 c. water
1 egg

To improve boxed-cake mixes, stir the first three ingredients into dry cake mix for a bigger and better cake. Prepare the cake mix as directed and add the water, egg, and vegetable oil, in addition.
Carolina J. Miller (Joni)

BLUEBERRY BUCKLE

1 1/4 c. sugar
1/4 c. shortening
2 eggs
1/2 c. milk
1 1/2 c. plus 1/3 c. flour
2 tsp. baking powder
1/2 tsp. salt

1/2 tsp. nutmeg
1/4 tsp. cloves
15 oz. (2 c.) blueberries
1/2 c. nuts
1/2 tsp. cinnamon
1/4 c. softened butter

Mix 3/4 c. sugar, shortening, eggs and milk until well blended. Stir in 1 1/2 c. flour, baking powder, salt, nutmeg and cloves. Fold in blueberries and spread batter into a 9"" square pan. Combine remaining ingredients and mix until crumbly. Sprinkle crumbs over batter and bake in preheated 375º oven for 45 min. to 50 min. or until top springs back when lightly touched. Serve warm and cut into squares. Serve with ice cream, whipped topping or cold milk
Yield: 9 servings
Aaron & Irene Miller

BUTTERMILK CHOCOLATE CAKE

Bring to a boil:
1 c. butter or 1/2 c. butter and
1/2 c. vegetable oil
2 T. cocoa
1 c. water

Sift together:
2 c. flour
2 c. sugar
1/2 tsp. salt
1 1/2 tsp. baking soda

Pour boiling ingredients on the dry mixture and stir together: Add 1/2 c. buttermilk, 1 tsp. vanilla, 2 beaten eggs. Mix together and bake at 350º.
Wayne & Kathryn Miller

BUTTERMILK CHOCOLATE CAKE ICING

3-4 T. cocoa
1/2 c. butter

6 T. buttermilk

Bring to a boil, remove from heat and add, 2 1/2 c. firmly packed powdered sugar, 1 tsp. vanilla, 1 c. nuts, if desired.
Yield: Enough for 1 cake
Wayne & Kathryn Miller

CAKE DIP

1 T. flour, rounded
1 c. sugar
1 T. butter

1 T. vanilla
1 tsp. vinegar
1 c. boiling water

Mix flour and some of the sugar with vinegar and vanilla. Stir into boiling water. Boil until thick. Add butter and the rest of the sugar. This is a delicious topping on chocolate cake with no icing. Eat with fresh strawberries.
Yield: 6 servings
Allen & Ruth Bontrager

CARAMEL FROSTING

1 stick butter
1 c. brown sugar
1/4 c. milk
1/4 tsp. salt

1 tsp. vanilla
1 c. powdered sugar
Chopped pecans

Melt the butter with the brown sugar and add the salt. Cook on low heat for two minutes. Take off the heat. Add the milk and vanilla, and beat in the powdered sugar. Beat well. Frost the cake before it's too cool. This is a good frosting. It takes less time and mixes well. It'll keep for a long time, also.
David & Mary Kauffman   Alva & Katie Ann Bontrager

The rooster may crow, but it's the hen who delivers the goods!

CARROT CAKE

3 eggs
1 c. vegetable oil
1 tsp. vanilla
2 c. flour
2 c. sugar
1/2 tsp. salt
1 tsp. baking soda
1 tsp. baking powder
2 tsp. cinnamon
2 c. carrots, finely grated
1 c. crushed pineapple, drained
1 c. coconut
1/2 c. nuts

Beat together the first three ingredients. Add the dry ingredients. Stir in carrots, pineapple, coconut and nuts. Pour into a greased 9 X 13 pan. Bake at 350º until cake tests done - approximately 50 minutes. Cream cheese frosting is great on this cake.
Yield:
David & Mary Kauffman

CARROT CAKE ICING

1 stick butter
1 - 8 oz. pkg. cream cheese
1 box (1 lb.) powdered sugar
1 tsp. vanilla

Blend butter and cream cheese until fluffy. Add powdered sugar and vanilla. Mix well. Enough for one 9 X 13 cake.

CHERRY STREUSEL CAKE

2 c. all-purpose flour
3/4 c. sugar
2 tsp. baking powder
1/4 tsp. salt
1 egg, beaten
1/2 c. milk
3/4 c. butter
Cherry pie filling

Streusel:

1/2 c. sugar
1/3 c. flour
1/4 c. butter
1 c. pecans

In a mixing bowl, combine flour, sugar, baking powder and salt. Add egg, milk and butter; beat well. Put 1/2 the batter in a 9 X 13 cake pan; spread cherry pie filling on this, then put the rest of the batter on top of the filling. Sprinkle streusel on top and bake at 350º until done.
Mary J. Miller (Joni)

When one door of happiness closes, another opens. But often we look so long at the closed door that we do not see the one that has been opened for us.

Getting rid of ourselves is like peeling an onion, layer by layer, and it is often a tearful process.

CHOCOLATE CHIFFON CAKE

3/4 c. boiling water
1/2 c. cocoa
1 3/4 c. cake flour
1 3/4 c. sugar
1 tsp. salt

1/2 c. oil
7 unbeaten egg yolks
1 tsp. vanilla
1 c. egg whites
1 tsp. cream of tartar

Stir together water and cocoa until smooth, and let cool. Sift flour, sugar, baking powder and salt into a bowl. Make a well and add in order - oil, egg yolks, cooled cocoa mixture and flavoring. Beat with a spoon until smooth. In a large bowl, beat egg whites and cream of tartar until very stiff peaks form. Pour batter mixture over the egg whites in a thin stream, gently cutting and folding it together. Pour into angel food pan. Bake at 325º for 10 minutes and finish baking at 350º.
Menno & Malinda Miller

CHOCOLATE CRAZY CAKE

3 c. flour
1/3 c. cocoa
2 tsp. baking soda
2 tsp. vanilla
2 c. cold water

2 c. sugar
1 tsp. salt
2 T. vinegar
3/4 c. oil

Mix dry ingredients. Add the liquid ingredients and stir. Do not beat. Pour into ungreased 9 X 13 pan. Bake at 350º for 35-40 minutes.
Yield: 6-8 servings
Aaron & Irene Miller

CHOCOLATE FUDGE CAKE

1/2 c. butter
1 1/2 c. sugar
2 lg. eggs
1 tsp. vanilla
1/2 c. plus 1 T. hot water
2/3 c. unsweetened cocoa

1 3/4 c. flour
1 tsp. soda
1 tsp. baking powder
1/2 tsp. salt
1 c. sour milk

To make cake - combine softened butter and sugar until fluffy, add eggs one at a time, beating well after each. Add vanilla. Stir hot water into cocoa to form a smooth paste, add to creamed mixture. Mix dry ingredients and add alternately with sour milk. Bake at 350º for 30-35 min.
Chocolate Cream Frosting - 3 sq. (3 oz.) unsweetened chocolate, 1 1/4 c. butter. Melt over low heat, stir to blend. Add 2 c. powdered sugar, 1/2 c. sour cream and 2 tsp. vanilla. Beat until smooth and creamy and spread on cooled cake.
Linda (Willis) Bontrager

CHOCOLATE UPSIDE DOWN CAKE

1 1/4 c. flour
3/4 c. sugar
2 tsp. baking powder
1/4 tsp. salt
3 T. cocoa

5 T. butter
1/2 c. milk
1 tsp. vanilla
1/2 c. nuts

Mix dry ingredients. Melt together chocolate and butter. Mix with milk and vanilla. Stir in dry ingredients thoroughly. Pour into an ungreased 8x10 cake pan. Mix together the following topping: 2 T. cocoa; 1/2 c. brown sugar; 1/2 c. white sugar; 1 c. boiling water. Pour over cake batter and bake for one hour. When slightly cooled, turn pan upside down on platter.
Menno & Malinda Miller

CHOCOLATE WONDER CAKE

2 1/4 c. flour
1/2 c. cocoa
1 1/2 tsp. baking soda
1 tsp. salt
1/2 c. shortening
1 c. sugar

1 tsp. vanilla
3 egg yolks
1 1/3 c. cold water
3 egg whites
3/4 c. sugar

Sift together first 4 ingredients. In another bowl, beat together, shortening, sugar and vanilla until very light and fluffy. Add egg yolks one at a time, beating well after each addition. Add dry ingredients and water alternately until well mixed. With clean beater, beat egg whites in small bowl until soft peaks form, gradually add the 3/4 c. sugar beating until stiff peaks form. Fold egg white mixture into batter. Blend well. I bake this in a tube pan at 350º for 30-35 min. or until done. We like to slice this cake and make ice cream sandwiches with it, because it's such a soft and moist cake.
Linda (Willis) Bontrager

COCONUT PECAN FROSTING

1 c. evaporated milk
1 c. sugar
3 egg yolks
1/4 lb. butter

1 tsp. vanilla
1 1/3 c. Angel Flake coconut
1 c. nuts, chopped (English walnuts or pecans)

Combine first five ingredients. Beat well. Cook and stir over medium heat for 12 minutes. Take from heat, add last two ingredients. Spread over cake while still warm. Spread over two 9 X 13 cake pans or three 8 to 9 round pans.

CREAM CHEESE CAKE

1 c. sour cream
1/2 c. sugar
1/2 c. margarine
1 teaspoon salt

2 pkgs. (1/4 oz.) dry yeast
1/2 c. warm water (110º to 115º)
2 eggs, beaten
4 c. flour

Filling:

2 pkg. (8 oz. each) cream
cheese, softened
3/4 c. sugar

1 egg, beaten
2 tsp. vanilla
1/8 tsp. salt

Glaze:

2 1/2 c. powdered sugar
1/4 c. milk

1 tsp. vanilla
Toasted sliced almonds

Combine sour cream, sugar, butter and salt. Cook over medium heat, stirring constantly, until well blended. Cool to room temperature. In a bowl, mix the yeast in water. Add this to the sour cream mixture. Gradually stir in flour. Cover and refrigerate overnight. Next day, mix the filling. Divide into four equal portions. Roll each portion into a 12x8 rectangle. Spread 1/4 of the filling on each to within one inch of the edges. Roll up jelly-roll style from the long side and pinch the seams and ends to seal. Place seam-side down on a greased baking sheet. Cut six x-marks on the top of the loaves. Cover and let rise until double in size. Bake at 375º for 20-25 minutes or until golden brown. Cool. Mix glaze, then drizzle over the loaves. Sprinkle with almonds. Store in the refrigerator.
Yield: 20-24 servings
Neal & Emma Yoder

DATE PUDDING CAKE

2 c. dates, cut fine
2 tsp. butter
1 1/2 c. boiling water
2 tsp. baking soda (in water)

2 c. brown sugar
2 eggs
3 1/2 c. flour

Mix first four ingredients. Stir in brown sugar and eggs. Add flour and mix well. Bake at 325º. Cut into cubes and cover with whipped cream or pudding and nuts.
Delilah Stoll

MONROE'S CAKE

2 c. sugar
1/2 c. butter
4 eggs
1 c. milk
Monroe W. Miller

3 c. flour
1/2 c. cocoa
6 tsp. baking powder
1 tsp. vanilla

EARTHQUAKE CAKE
1 c. coconut
1 c. chocolate chips
1 c. nuts
1 box yellow cake mix

1 stick butter
8 oz. cream cheese
4 c. powdered sugar

Grease sides and bottom of a 9 X 13 pan. Sprinkle coconut, chocolate chips and nuts on bottom. Make cake as directed on package. Pour on top of nut mixture. Cream butter, cream cheese and add 1 c. powdered sugar at a time until all is used up. Very carefully spoon this on top of the unbaked cake. Bake at 350º for 1 hour. May put cool whip on top.
Paul & Rhonda Borkholder

FAVORITE SHORTCAKE
2 c. flour
3 tsp. baking powder
3/4 tsp. salt
1 T. sugar
1/3 c. shortening
2/3 c. milk

1 egg beaten
Topping:
1/2 c. sugar
1/2 c. flour
3 T. butter

Mix the first five ingredients into crumbs. Add milk and egg. Pour into a small cake pan. Mix topping ingredients together until crumbly. Sprinkle on top of batter. Bake at 350º for 35 minutes.
Yield: 6 servings
Amos & Elizabeth Miller

FRIENDSHIP CAKE
1/3 c. flour
1/3 c. sugar

1/3 c. milk

Don't refrigerate; cover with lid. Days 1-2-3-4 stir. Day 5 add:
1 c. flour
1 c. sugar

1 c. milk

Days 6-7-8-9 stir. Day 10 add:
1 c. flour
1 c. sugar

1 c. milk

Stir and take out 1 c. for each of 3 friends. To the remaining add:
2/3 c. vegetable oil
3 eggs
1 c. sugar
2 c. flour
1 1/2 tsp. cinnamon

1 1/2 tsp. baking soda
1/2 tsp. salt
2 tsp. baking powder
2 tsp. vanilla

Topping:
1 c. brown sugar
1/2 stick butter

1 tsp. flour

Nuts, raisins, crushed pineapple, etc. can be added.
Barbara Miller

GINGERBREAD

1 c. sugar
1 c. butter
4 eggs, beaten
2 tsp. baking soda, dissolved in
1 c. hot water

1 c. molasses
1 tsp. nutmeg
1 tsp. cinnamon
5 c. flour

Beat together sugar, butter and eggs. Add liquids. Mix dry stuff together and mix everything together. Bake in 9 X 13 pan at 350º for 30 min. This is especially good with whipped cream on top while still warm.
Linda (Willis) Bontrager

GRANDMA'S CRUMB CAKE

4 c. flour
1 c. lard
1 c. white sugar

1 tsp. baking soda
Pinch of salt

Mix these ingredients into a crumb texture.
1 1/2 c. molasses
1 1/2 c. hot water

1 tsp. baking soda

Pour this in a pan and put crumbs on top.
Grandma Emma Miller

LONG JOHNS

2 T. yeast, dissolved in
1 c. warm water
1 c. lukewarm milk (scald then cool)
1/2 c. butter
2/3 c. sugar
     Filling:
1 c. milk
4 T. flour

2 eggs
1/2 tsp. salt
Vanilla
6 - 7 c. flour

Pinch of salt

     Cook together then let get cold. Combine:
1/2 c. butter
1/2 c. Crisco

1 T. vanilla

Add powdered sugar until right consistency, approximately 2 lb.
Linda (Willis) Bontrager

MARSHMALLOW TOPPING

2 c. white sugar
2 1/2 c. light Karo

1 c. water

Cook to 253º then cool 5 min. Add 7/8 c. egg whites (3/4 c. plus 1 egg white = 7/8 c.) beaten stiff and 1/2 c. Karo. Stir. Vanilla may be added if you wish.
Mabel (DeVon) Miller

MAPLE NUT CHIFFON CAKE

2 c. all-purpose flour
3/4 c. white sugar
3/4 c. brown sugar
1 T. baking powder
1 tsp. salt
1/2 c. salad oil

7 egg yolks
3/4 c. cold water
2 tsp. maple flavoring
7 egg whites
1/2 tsp. cream of tartar
1 c. finely chopped nuts

In a large bowl, stir dry ingredients thoroughly. Make a well and add, in order, the salad oil, yolks, cold water and maple flavoring. Stir until smooth. In large bowl of electric mixer, beat egg whites with cream of tartar until stiff peaks form. Gradually pour egg yolk mixture over egg whites. Fold gently until just blended. Gently fold in nuts. Pour into an angel food baking pan and bake for 1 hour.
Yield: 1 cake
Wayne & Kathryn Miller

MONKEY BREAD

3 cans refrigerated biscuits,
    10 count each
3/4 c. sugar
1 1/2 tsp. cinnamon
1/2 c. nuts, optional

Topping:
3/4 c. butter or margarine
1 c. sugar
1 1/4 tsp. cinnamon

Cut each biscuit in quarters and shake in mixture of sugar and cinnamon. Drop into bundt pan. Sprinkle with nuts. In a small pan, combine topping ingredients and bring to a boil. Pour over biscuits in the pan and bake at 350º for 40-45 minutes. Turn out right away on a plate when done. Delicious! Perfect for coffee breaks.
Glen & Sue Ellen Borkholder

OATMEAL CAKE

1 c. oatmeal
1 1/4 c. water
1 1/2 c. brown sugar
1/2 c. oil
1 egg

1 tsp. baking powder
1 tsp. baking soda
1/2 tsp. salt
2 tsp. cinnamon
1 tsp. vanilla

1 1/3 c. cake flour (we use 1/2 spelt or wheat flour)
        Frosting:
1 1/2 c. brown sugar
1 c. coconut
1 c. nuts

6 T. butter, melted
1/4 c. cream

Mix the oatmeal and water together and let set. Mix in the remaining ingredients and bake at 350º. Then top with frosting and brown lightly in broiler.
Joni & Emma Sue Miller

OATMEAL PONE

2 c. rolled oats
1 c. whole wheat flour
1/2 c. brown sugar, or less
1 tsp. baking soda

1 tsp. salt
1 egg
1 1/4 - 1 1/2 c. milk, cream or
buttermilk, etc.

Blend dry ingredients together. Add the egg and milk. Bake in an 8 square pan in a moderate oven, approximately 30 minutes or until done. This simple, homey cake is very good served with berries, cherries, or fresh peaches and milk. Variation: Adding about a cup of finely chopped apples makes a nice addition.
Urie & Lizzie Ann Miller

PENUCHE ICING

1/2 c. butter
1 c. brown sugar, packed

1/4 c. milk
1 3/4 - 2 c. confectioner's sugar

Melt butter in saucepan. Add brown sugar. Boil over low heat 2 minutes. Stir in milk - bring to a boil stirring constantly. Cool to lukewarm. Gradually add powdered sugar. Beat until thick enough to spread. If icing becomes too stiff, add a little hot water.
Ivan & Martha Miller

PINEAPPLE FROSTING

1 pkg. Cool Whip
1 box instant vanilla pudding

1 can crushed pineapple

Mix all ingredients together and spread on cake. This is great on angel food cake.
Delilah Stoll

PUMPKIN PIE CAKE

1 lg. can evaporated milk
1 lg. can pumpkin (3 c.)
1 1/2 c. sugar

3 tsp. pumpkin pie spice
3 eggs

Beat above ingredients together. Pour into a 9 X 13 cake pan. Sprinkle one large pkg. of yellow cake mix over the mixture in the cake pan and sprinkle walnuts on top. Drizzle 1 1/2 cubes melted butter on top. When cold, top with Rich's topping. Bake at 350º.
Yield: 9 X 13 cake pan
Mary J. Miller (Joni)

He who relates the faults of others to you, designs to relate yours to others. Scandal always runs best in the gutter of evil minds.

PUMPKIN SHEET CAKE

2 c. sugar
1 c. vegetable oil
4 eggs, lightly beaten
2 c. all-purpose flour
2 tsp. ground cinnamon
1/2 tsp. salt

Frosting:
1 pkg. (3 oz.) cream cheese, softened
5 T. butter, softened
1 tsp. vanilla
1 3/4 c. confectioner's sugar
3-4 tsp. milk
Chopped nuts

In a mixing bowl, beat pumpkin, sugar and oil. Add eggs; mix well. Combine flour, baking soda, cinnamon and salt; add to pumpkin mixture and beat until well blended. Pour into a greased 15 X 10x1 baking pan. Bake at 350º for 25-30 minutes or until cake tests done. Cool. For the frosting, beat the cream cheese, butter and vanilla until smooth. Gradually add sugar, then milk. Put on cake. Sprinkle nuts on top.
Yield: 20-24 servings
Neal & Emma Yoder

RHUBARB CAKE DESSERT

Crumble together and press into a cake pan:
1/2 lb. butter   1/2 c. sugar
2 c. flour
         Custard:
5 c. rhubarb   1 c. cream
6 egg yolks   1/4 tsp. salt
2 c. sugar   1 c. milk
4 T. flour
         Meringue:
6 egg whites, beaten   2 T. vanilla
1/2 c. sugar   Pinch of salt

Bake the custard at 350º for 40-45 minutes. A little before the custard is done, pour meringue on top of custard and bake until golden brown on top.
Yield: 12 servings
Mary J. Miller (Joni)   Sammie & Kathryn Schrock

SHOO FLY PIE OR CAKE

4 c. flour   In a dish, put:
1 c. lard   1/2 c. molasses
1 c. sugar   2 c. hot water
1 tsp. baking soda   1 tsp. baking soda
Pinch of salt

Stir until baking soda dissolves. Quickly put on crumbs and bake at 350º - 375º.
Delilah Stoll (From Grandma Emma Miller)

SALAD DRESSING CHOCOLATE CAKE

3 1/2 c. sifted flour
2 c. sugar
3 T. cocoa
1 1/2 tsp. baking powder
1 1/2 tsp. baking soda
1/4 tsp. salt
2 c. salad dressing
2 c. water
1 T. vanilla

Mix the first six ingredients. Add the remaining ingredients and mix well. Pour batter into a 9 X 13 pan. Bake at 350º until done in center. This is a good cake to use old salad dressing, and also for people who are watching their fat. It stays moist for a long time.
Yield: 1 cake
Alva & Katie Ann Bontrager

SUPPER CAKE

1/2 c. shortening
1 egg
1 1/2 c. sugar
1 c. milk
3 c. flour
3 tsp. baking powder
1/4 tsp. salt
Rhubarb or other fruit

Cut enough rhubarb (or other fruit) to cover the bottom of the pan. Sprinkle with 1 c. sugar and dot with butter. Pour the batter over the top and bake. Add sugar and milk at the table.
Yield: 10 servings
Monroe & Elsie Miller

TURTLE CAKE

1 c. sugar
1 c. salad dressing
1 c. warm water
2 tsp. baking soda
1 tsp. vanilla
1/2 tsp. salt
2 c. flour
1/3 c. cocoa
1/2 c. butter
1 - 14 oz. pkg. caramels
1 can Eagle Brand milk
3/4 c. chopped pecans
3/4 c. chocolate chips

Beat together sugar and salad dressing, add baking soda to warm water and pour in first mixture. Add vanilla. Sift dry ingredients together and add gradually to other mixture. Bake half of this batter in a 9 X 13 pan for 15 min. Meanwhile, melt butter, caramels and milk in top of double boiler until melted. Remove from heat. Cool slightly and pour over baked half of cake. Pour remaining batter on top. Sprinkle with pecans and chips. Bake for 25 min. at 350º. Delicious with ice cream.
Yield: 9 X 13 pan
Linda (Willis) Bontrager

Brush just the teeth you want to keep.

WACKY CAKE

3 c. flour
2 c. sugar
1 tsp. salt
2 tsp. baking soda
2 tsp. baking powder
6 T. cocoa

10 T. oil
2 c. lukewarm water
2 T. vinegar
Vanilla
Salt

Sift the dry ingredients together and add the oil to it. Add and mix the rest of the ingredients together and pour into a 9 X 13 cake pan. Bake until done.
Sam & Ruby Miller

WHITE CAKE

1/2 c. shortening
1/2 c. butter
2 c. sugar
1 tsp. lemon
3 c. sifted flour
4 tsp. baking powder

1 1/2 c. milk
6 beaten egg whites
1 tsp. vanilla
Vanilla
Pinch of salt
Dash of Lemon

Cream the shortening and butter together. Add the rest of the ingredients. Mix and bake at 350º until done.
Sam & Ruby Miller   Delilah Stoll

WHITE ICING

1 egg white
1 c. sugar
1/2 c. Crisco
1/2 c. butter

3/4 c. hot milk
1 tsp. vanilla
Pinch of salt

Beat egg whites until stiff. Gradually add sugar - a tablespoon at a time. Add the Crisco and butter. Beat until fluffy. Add hot milk - a tablespoon at a time. Beat well - egg beater works well. Add vanilla and salt.
Ella E. Miller

ZUCCHINI SQUASH CAKE

3 c. zucchini, peeled and grated
2 c. sugar
4 eggs
1 c. vegetable oil
3 c. flour

1 tsp. soda
1 tsp. vanilla
2 tsp. baking powder
1/2 tsp. salt
1 c. nuts

Combine first four ingredients. Add dry ingredients next, then nuts and vanilla. Bake at 350º for 40-45 minutes.
Yield: 12-14 servings

CANDY

Peanut Brittle.

2 cups Sugar
1 cup white Karo
1 cup water
cook till it forms a
hard Ball in cold water
now add 4 cups unroast
Peanuts, 1 tea sp Butter
cook till golden Brown
not dark. Stir all the time
Take from fire add 1 tea
sp vanilla 2 tea sp
soda stir fast has
your sheets greased
Before hand, quickly
Pour and scrape out
on sheets. let get cold
you can break it in
pieces

Emma

Original Recipe

BAKED CARMEL CORN

1/2 c. margarine
2 c. brown sugar
1/2 c. sorghum syrup

Boil above for 5 minutes and add:
3/4 tsp. baking soda
2 tsp. vanilla

Pour over 6-8 qt. popped corn in greased mixing bowl. Put in oven at 250º for 30 minutes, stirring every 10 minutes. Pack in containers as soon as cool. They'll keep crisp.
Delilah Stoll

CARAMELS

1 c. white sugar
3/4 c. white Karo
1/2 c. cream
1/4 lb. butter

1/2 c. evaporated milk
1/2 tsp. vanilla
Pecans, optional

Mix sugar, corn syrup, and cream. Boil to 230º on thermometer. Add evaporated milk in a small stream so as not to stop boiling, milk may curdle. Slow fire, add butter and salt. Stir vigorously as milk and cream scorch easily. Cook 244º or test it in water until a firm ball. Remove from heat. Add desired amount of pecans. Pour into buttered 9 cake pan, may add chocolate on top. Can also be used for turtles. Best way to test caramels is to put some caramels in cold water (not ice) and flatten. When cool it should be the firmness you want.
Ella E. Miller

BUCKEYES

1 lbs. peanut butter
1 1/2 lb. powdered sugar

2 sticks butter (1 c.)

Roll in balls and let chill. Dip in melted chocolate.
Yield: 3 lbs.
Aaron & Irene Miller

BUNS

8 oz. cream cheese
8 oz. butter

9 c. powdered sugar
1 tsp. maple flavor

Mix together and set in cold, then roll out between plastic about 1/3" thick, cut in rounds and dip in chocolate, then put a tsp. of peanuts and chocolate mixed on top. I like the dry roasted Planters peanuts for this.
Linda (Willis) Bontrager

BUTTERMILK FUDGE

2 c. buttermilk   2 tsp. baking soda (scant)

Mix together in large saucepan and let stand 3-5 minutes. Add 4 cups sugar and 1 scant cup butter (unsalted). Mix. Boil together until soft ball stage; stirring constantly. Cool until your hand can easily stand to touch bottom of pan. Add vanilla and nuts (if desired). Beat until it loses its shine and becomes creamy. Put in buttered pan and cut into bite-size pieces. Very good eating!

Delilah Stoll

CHOCOLATE CLUSTERS

2 lb. white chocolate   2 c. salted dry roasted peanuts
1 c. peanut butter   4 c. Rice Krispies

Melt white chocolate and peanut butter, stirring often to mix. Add the rest and drop by spoonfuls on waxed paper.

Linda (Willis) Bontrager

CHOCOLATE PEANUT BALLS

4 c. crunchy peanut butter   6 oz. chocolate chips
6 c. Rice Krispies   1/4 lb. paraffin, optional
1 1/2 lbs. powdered sugar

Mix, by hand, the first four ingredients. Form into balls. Melt chocolate and paraffin in a double boiler. Dip the balls into the chocolate and set on wax paper.

Yield: 80 balls

Jacob & Loretta Shetler

PEANUT BRITTLE

2 c. sugar   1 tsp. butter
1 c. white Karo   1 tsp. vanilla
1 c. water   2 tsp. baking soda
4 c. unroasted peanuts

Cook the sugar, Karo and water until it forms a hard ball in cold water. Now add unroasted peanuts and butter. Cook until a golden brown color, not dark. Stir all the time. Take from the heat and add vanilla and baking soda. Stir fast. Have your baking sheets greased before hand. Quickly pour and scrape out brittle mixture onto the sheets. Let it get cold and then break into pieces.

Yield: 5 lbs.

Grandma Emma Miller

Can it be an accident that "stressed" is "desserts" spelled backwards?!

PEANUT BUTTER CUPS

1 1/2 c. powdered sugar
2 c. peanut butter
1/4 c. butter, melted
1/4 c. Carnation canned milk
1 T. vanilla
1/2 tsp. salt
Cool then make into balls and dip into chocolate.
Linda (Willis) Bontrager

PEPPERMINT CANDY

1 - 13 oz. jar marshmallow cream
3 T. Crisco, rounded
1 1/4 lb. powdered sugar
3/4 tsp. peppermint oil
English walnuts
Mix everything together well. Peppermint will taste stronger when set overnight. I add coarse chopped walnuts as thick as I want them. Roll in balls and let set overnight. Next day dip in chocolate.
Linda (Willis) Bontrager

TAFFY

1 pt. Karo
1 qt. white sugar
1 pt. Cream
Paraffin the size of a walnut
2 tsp. vanilla
     Boil the above to a hard ball stage then add:
1 T. gelatin
1/4 c. water
Pour in buttered pans and cool. Then 2 people to a pan and pull until nice and white. Cut in small pieces and wrap into wax paper. Some of you cousins will remember the taffy pulls we had at our house, playing games until the taffy was ready. What wonderful memories. This was the recipe we used.
Linda (Willis) Bontrager   David & Mary Kauffman

VANILLA TARTS

1 c. sugar
1 c. maple syrup
1 egg
1 pt. water
2 c. sugar
1 c. sour milk or sour cream
2 eggs
1 tsp. baking soda
1/2 c. lard
3 c. flour
1 tsp. vanilla
Put first four ingredients in 9 X 13 baking pan. Mix together sugar, eggs, lard, baking soda, flour, vanilla and milk. Put this mixture on top of the syrup. May also be put in unbaked pie shell for 4 pies. Bake at 350º until done.
Ivan & Martha Miller

Faith is. . . remembering I am God's priceless treasure when I feel simply worthless.

CANNING, FREEZING & PRESERVING

A Special Greeting For You!

48

BANANA PICKLES

3 c. sugar
1 c. vinegar
1 c. water
1 tsp. salt

1 tsp. celery seed
1 tsp. mustard seed
1 tsp. turmeric

Peel big cucumbers. Scoop out seeds. Cut in spears and pack spears in jars. Cover with the vinegar mixture. Cold pack for 5 min. after water boils.
Mabel (DeVon) Miller

CHUNKY PIZZA SAUCE TO CAN

I peel all tomatoes and chunk up. Put in about 2 qt. tomatoes to start with. Put on burner and let them simmer and add seasonings. I do not strain my tomatoes. Use a 12 qt. kettle:

2 T. oregano
1 T. garlic salt
1/2 T. red pepper
2 T. salt
3 T. Lawry's season salt
2 T. brown sugar, heaping
1/2 c. southwest pizza seasoning

3 T. fresh cilantro, cut up or 1 T. coriander
1 qt. onions, cut up
1-2 qt. peppers, cut up
2 c. tomato paste
1 1/2 c. oil

Let this simmer awhile then fill kettle up with tomato chunks, simmer for 1/2 hr. Thicken with clear jell. Put in jars and cold pack. The cilantro looks like celery leaves and you can get it fresh on produce line in most stores. This puts that Mexican zest into your sauce. You can substitute coriander, but I don't like it as well.
Linda (Willis) Bontrager

MINCEMEAT

4 lbs. beef meat
3 lbs. suet
1/2 lb. citron
3 lbs. brown sugar
3 lbs. currants
3 lbs. raisins

9 lbs. apples
3 qt. Cider
1/2 lb. candied orange peel
1/4 lb. candied lemon peel
4 oranges
2 lemons

1 oz. Each of mase, nutmeg, cinnamon and cloves
Cover meat with water and cook until tender. Cut fine. Add suet (chopped fine), sugar, currants and raisins and the other fruits. Cook over a low fire until the apples are tender and can. Eat as is or use for pies.

For fresh tasting vegetables add 1 T. lemon juice and salt per qt..

SPAGHETTI SAUCE TO CAN

13 qt. tomato juice
3 c. onions, ground
6 lg. green peppers
2 c. celery, ground
1/3 c. salt
1 c. sugar
1/2 c. oil
2 T. pepper
2 tsp. basil
2 tsp. garlic powder
3 pkg. spaghetti sauce mix
2 tsp. thyme
2 tsp. oregano

Cook together for three hours, then add two large cans tomato paste and 1 - 8 oz. can parmesan cheese. Stir often.
Joni & Emma Sue Miller

SPAGHETTI SAUCE TO CAN

1/2 bu. tomatoes
4 peppers
3 lbs. onions
2 c. salad oil
1/3 c. sugar
1/2 c. salt
2 T. basil
1 T. oregano
4 T. parsley flakes
3 cloves garlic
1 bunch celery
4 - 12 oz. cans tomato paste

Cook tomatoes 3 hours then strain. Chop onions, celery, peppers and garlic and add to the mixture along with salt, sugar, basil, oregano, and parsley. Mix salad oil with tomato paste and a small amount of tomato juice, and add to cooked tomatoes. Cook all together on medium heat for 1 hour, then bring to a boil. Fill canning jars and seal.
Paul & Rhonda Borkholder

VEGETABLE SOUP TO CAN

4 qt. peas, fresh or frozen
3 qt. green beans, cooked and cut fine
4 qt. carrots, sliced and cooked
2 qt. onions, chopped
6 qt. potatoes, cooked and cut fine
6 qt. canned chunks or frozen steaks
Large skillet of beef gravy
2 can hot tomato juice
2 big cans of cream of chicken soup
Add tomato juice enough what you want
I like to freeze steaks when we butcher, then fry and make into small pieces; this makes the best flavor. I flavor and season all my vegetables as I cook them, then with the hot tomato juice and cream of chicken it makes a good flavor.
Yield: over 30 qt.
Linda (Willis) Bontrager

STRAWBERRIES TO CAN

4 c. sugar   4 qt. strawberries, mashed
1 c. water
4 T. Clear Jell, Perma Flo or cornstarch
Mix the first three ingredients and then add the strawberries. Bring to a boil and then ladle into hot jars and seal.
Yield: 4 qt.
Monroe & Elsie Miller   Allen & Ruth Bontrager

KEEPING APPLES

To keep apples for the winter, put them in a black garbage bag with one cup of water. Be sure to get all the air out and tie the bag with a twist tie to close.
Amos & Elizabeth Miller

SYRUP FOR FRUITS

Thin Syrup - 1 part sugar to 3 parts water
Medium Syrup - 1 part sugar to 2 parts water
Thick Syrup - 1 part sugar to 1 part water
Sammie & Kathryn Schrock

MEATLOAF TO CAN

15 lbs. hamburger	2 c. tomato juice
1/4 c. salt	1/2 c. brown sugar
1 long pack crackers	2 tsp. pepper
2 med. onions	1/4 c. parsley
1 1/2 c. oatmeal	Oregano
2 c. water	Garlic salt

Mix all the ingredients together. Pack into jars and cold pack for three hours, or pressure cook at 10 lb. for one hour. (Do not fill jars too full as oatmeal expands.)
Joni & Emma Sue Miller

PORK AND BEANS TO CAN

8 lbs. dry beans	1/2 tsp. red pepper
2 lbs. browned bacon or beef	1 tsp. dry mustard
3 c. water	1 tsp. cinnamon
4 qt. tomato juice	1 lg. onion
3 c. white sugar	1 1/2 bottle of ketchup
4 c. brown sugar	

Cook the dried beans till fairly soft. Mix the remaining ingredients with beans. Put in jars and process to seal.
Yield:

CHERRY PIE FILLING TO CAN

8 c. pitted, tart cherries   1/8 c. cherry Jello
6 c. sugar   1 tsp. almond flavoring
1 1/2 c. Perma Flo

Mix cherries and three c. sugar and let set overnight. Next day drain the cherries and use the juice with enough water added to make eight c.. Bring water to a boil. Mix Perma Flo and three c. sugar together. Add enough water to make a paste. Add to the boiling water. Cook for ten minutes on low heat. Add cherries, flavoring and Jello. Bring to a boil. Put into jars. Put jars in a water bath and cook for ten minutes.
Yield: 4 qt.
Amos & Elizabeth Miller

BACON CURE

To cure bacon use two oz. tenderquick, 2 oz. sugar cure and 15 lbs. of bacon. Sprinkle tenderquick and sugar cure over bacon. Two oz. equals 1/3 cup scant and not packed either.

BOLOGNA TIP

If bologna is cold packed 2-3 hours instead of pressure cooked, it won't be so dry.

BRINE FOR HAM

2 rounded c. Tenderquick   1/2 c. Liquid Smoke
5 qt. water   2 T. black pepper
3 c. brown sugar

Make enough brine to cover ham. Trim bacon and ham before putting in the brine. Dissolve and pour over raw ham slices. More water may be needed. Weight slices so all is covered with liquid. Cure bacon 14 days, cure ham 5 days and then freeze, can, or bake whole. Delicious frozen and then grilled.
Yield:
Oba & Laura Borkholder   Glen & Sue Ellen Borkholder

To soften hardened sugar, put it in the freezer or add a piece of bread in an enclosed container.

Wash off the clothesline with vinegar to keep wash from freezing onto the line.

CHILDREN'S SECTION

Hello!
Happy Birthday!

BROWNIES

1 yellow (or lemon) cake mix   2 eggs
1/2 c. oil   6 oz. (or less) chocolate chips
Stir ingredients all together. Pour into cookie sheet or cake pan.
Bake at 350º about 15 minutes or until light brown. Cool and cut in
bars.
Yield: 12 squares
Allen & Ruth Bontrager

COCOA DROP COOKIES (UNBAKED)

Boil together 5 minutes: 1/2 c. butter
2 c. white sugar   1 tsp. vanilla
1/2 c. cocoa powder   1 c. peanut butter, (optional)
1/2 c. milk
Mix well with 3 c. quick oats. Drop by spoonfuls on waxed paper
and cool.
Nancy Stoll, age 6

EASY SALSA

4 medium tomatoes, chopped   1/2 tsp. Salt
1 medium onion, chopped   1/4 tsp. Pepper
1/4 c. chunky salsa
1/4 c. canned chopped green chilies (optional)
Combine all ingredients, cover and refrigerate for several hours.
Yield: 5 c.

FINGER JELLO

3 1/2 T. gelatin   3 c. boiling water
2 tsp. lemon juice   1 1/2 c. any flavor Jello
Pour boiling water over Jello and stir until dissolved. Add lemon
juice and pour into pans. When Jello has set, cut into squares or
use cookie cutters to make fancy designs. Happy eating!
Menno & Malinda Miller

One tablespoon of sulfur put into the stove will stop, almost
instantly, the worst stovepipe fire or chimney fire. If a tablespoon
of sulfur is put in the stove each week, the pipes on the heater or
cookstove will rarely have to be taken down and cleaned. Tin cans
burned in the stove will also work to help keep your chimney clean.

See also section "Homemade Toys & Games"

FLAP JACK CAKE

1 c. sugar
1/4 tsp. salt
4 c. flour

8 tsp. baking powder
2 tsp. vanilla
1 c. milk or more

Mix ingredients in the order given. Add milk until mixture reaches a nice dough consistency and then put in a pan. Sprinkle with brown sugar and cinnamon to taste. Bake at 350º for 30 minutes. Serve with milk.
Yield: Makes a large cake
Sammie & Kathryn Schrock

FRUIT POPS

1 package 3 oz. Gelatin (any flavor)
1/2 c. sugar
2 c. boiling water
1 1/2 c. cold water
10-12 Popsicle molds or paper cups (3 oz.)
10-12 Popsicle sticks or plastic spoons
In a heat resistant bowl, dissolve gelatin and sugar in boiling water. Stir in cold water. Pour into molds or paper cups. Freeze for 2 hours or until almost firm. Insert sticks or spoons. Freeze 8 hours.

HALF HOUR PUDDING

1 c. flour
1 c. raisins
1/2 c. brown sugar
        Sauce:
3/4 c. brown sugar
2 T. butter

2 T. lard
1 tsp. baking powder
1/2 c. sweet milk

2 c. boiling water

Mix the first six ingredients together in the order given and put in a pan. For the sauce, stir all ingredients until dissolved, then pour over the batter. Don't stir! Bake at 350º.
Yield: 6 servings
Sammie & Kathryn Schrock

UNBAKE COOKIES

1/2 c. butter
4 c. sugar, or less

2 T. cocoa
1 c. milk

Mix together and stir constantly over high heat for 5 minutes or until butter melts. Remove and add 1 c. peanut butter, if desired. Add 6 c. oatmeal and mix well - press into a greased pan and chill. Cut before it gets too cold.
Wayne & Kathryn Miller

MOM'S LETTER CAKE

1 c. sour cream (heavy)
2 eggs
2 c. brown sugar
Beat very well, then add: 1/2 c. sweet milk
Yield: 1 cake
Elnora Stoll

MUNCH A "BIRD NEST"

6 c. Rice Krispies
6 c. corn flakes
2 c. coconut
1 1/2 c. brown sugar

2 c. Karo
2 c. peanut butter
2 tsp. butter
1 tsp. vanilla

Combine dry ingredients in a bowl. Mix the wet ingredients and bring just to a boil. Remove from heat and stir in cereal mixture. Let it cool then shape into bird nests. Fill with jelly beans, Milk Duds or other round candy eggs. This is also a neat birthday treat to press in the bottom of a pie pan and fill with ice cream pie.
Yield: 4 doz. balls
Jacob & Loretta Shetler

SNOWBALLS

Step 1: Mix
1/2 c. peanut butter
1/2 c. Rice Krispies
1/2 c. icing sugar

Step 2:
Dissolve in separate bowl
1 c. icing sugar
2 T. water

Step 3:
Coconut

After mixing ingredients in step 1, form small balls. Dip balls in dissolved icing sugar to coat them. Last roll them in coconut. Cool 20 min.
Enoch Stoll, age 8

WESSON OIL CAKE

3 1/2 c. sifted flour
2 c. sugar
1 tsp. salt
2 tsp. baking soda
2 T. cocoa

1 c. Wesson oil
2 c. cold water
2 T. vinegar
2 tsp. vanilla

Sift the flour and mix the ingredients in the order given. Bake at 350º.
Yield: 9 X 13 Pan
Allen & Ruth Bontrager

APPLESAUCE OATMEAL COOKIES

1 1/2 c. shortening
2 c. brown sugar
1 c. white sugar
2 eggs
2 tsp. vanilla
2 c. applesauce

3 c. flour
2 tsp. salt
2 tsp. cinnamon
2 tsp. baking soda
6 c. oatmeal

Cream the shortening and sugars, add the eggs and vanilla. Blend in applesauce. Add the dry ingredients and stir well. Drop onto cookie sheet. Bake at 350º.
Yield: Approx. 3 doz.
David & Mary Kauffman

BLACK WALNUT COOKIES

1 c. black walnuts, crushed
1 c. brown sugar
1 beaten egg

1/3 c. flour
1/8 tsp. salt
1/8 tsp. baking soda

Sift flour, salt and baking soda together. Mix egg and brown sugar. Blend in dry ingredients. Add walnuts (the walnuts are the shortening). Bake on a greased cookie sheet for 15 minutes at 350º.
Yield: 2 doz.
Wilma M. Miller

BLACK BOTTOM BANANA BARS

1/2 c. butter, softened
1 c. sugar
1 egg
1 tsp. vanilla extract
1 1/2 c. mashed ripe bananas

1 1/2 c. all-purpose flour
1 tsp. baking powder
1 tsp. baking soda
1/2 tsp. salt
1/4 c. baking cocoa

In a mixing bowl, cream butter and sugar. Add egg and vanilla. Beat until thoroughly combined. Blend in the bananas. Combine the flour, baking powder, baking soda and salt. Add to creamed mixture and mix well. Divide batter in half. Add cocoa to half; spread into greased 13x9 baking pan. Spoon remaining batter on top and swirl with a knife. Bake at 350º for 25 min. or until bars test done. Cool.
Yield: 2 1/2 - 3 doz.

It is bad to suppress laughter - It goes back down and spreads to your hips!

CAKE MIX COOKIES

1 box cake mix, dry
4 1/2 T. oil
2 eggs

Bake at 350º, but don't over bake. Delicious! Cover with your favorite frosting, if desired.
Yield:
Mary J. Miller (Joni)

CHEWY OATMEAL COOKIES

3 c. brown sugar
4 eggs, beaten
1 1/2 c. butter
1 1/2 tsp. baking soda
1 tsp. salt
2 tsp. cinnamon
2 tsp. vanilla
2 1/2 c. flour
4 c. quick oatmeal

Wayne & Kathryn Miller

CHEWY OATMEAL COOKIES FILLING

2 egg whites
1 tsp. vanilla
2 c. powdered sugar
1 1/2 c. Crisco, scant

Beat egg whites until stiff. Add the rest of the ingredients and blend together.
Wayne & Kathryn Miller

CHERRY CHEWBILEES

Crust:
1 1/4 c. flour
1/2 c. packed brown sugar
1/2 c. butter Crisco

1 c. chopped walnuts, divided
1/2 c. flaked coconut

Filling:
2 pkg. cream cheese, softened
2/3 c. sugar
2 eggs
2 tsp. vanilla
2 can (21 oz. each) cherry pie filling (or make your own)

In a bowl, combine flour and brown sugar; cut in shortening until fine crumbs form. Stir in 1/2 c. nuts and coconut. Reserve 1/2 c. crumb mixture for topping. Press remaining mixture into a 9 X 13 buttered pan. Bake at 350º for 12-15 min. or until lightly browned. Meanwhile, for filling, beat cream cheese, sugar, eggs and vanilla in a mixing bowl until smooth. Spread over hot crust. Bake 15 min. Spread pie filling on top, combine remaining nuts and crumbs, sprinkle over cherries. Bake 15 min. more. Try and not let crust get too hard (over baked).
Yield: 9 x 13 pan
Linda (Willis) Bontrager

CHOCOLATE CHIP COOKIES
2 c. brown sugar
1 c. white sugar
1 c. shortening or Butter-Flavor Crisco
1 c. margarine or Butter-Flavor Crisco
6 eggs
1 T. vanilla
2 tsp. salt, scant
4 tsp. baking soda
4 tsp. cream of tartar
7 c. sifted flour
1 sm. box instant vanilla pudding
1 pkg. chocolate chips
Chopped nuts, if desired
Mix all dry ingredients together. Mix well in order given. Drop b y teaspoon on cookie sheet. Bake at 350º for 10-12 min. for a chewy cookie. Take out after 8 min. and let set on pan for a couple minutes.
Yield: 4 doz.
Barbara Miller Raymond & Martha Bontrager

CHOCOLATE CHIP OATMEAL BAR
Beat together:
1/2 c. butter   1/2 c. brown sugar
1/2 c. white sugar   1 tsp. vanilla
          Add:
1 beaten egg   1 tsp. baking soda
1 3/4 c. quick oatmeal   1/2 tsp. cinnamon
1 c. flour   3/4 c. chopped nuts
Mix well. Spread into a 9 X 13 pan. Bake at 350º for 25 minutes; just until the center is set. Sprinkle 1 c. chocolate chips on top. Leave in oven 5 min. until chips are shiny. Take out and spread smoothly over the top.
Yield: 9 x 13 pan
Ruby Miller

Women: Remember, as we get older, we are no longer having hot flashes. They are now called power surges!

He's on a garlic diet. He hasn't lost any weight, but quite a few friends.

CHOCOLATE MARSHMALLOW BARS

3/4 c. butter
1 1/2 c. sugar
3 eggs
1 tsp. vanilla
1 1/2 c. flour
Topping:
1 1/3 c. (8 oz.) chocolate chips
3 T. butter

1/2 tsp. baking powder
1/2 tsp. salt
3 T. cocoa
1/2 c. nuts, chopped
4 c. mini-marshmallows

1 c. peanut butter
2 c. crisp rice cereal

In a mixing bowl, cream butter and sugar. Add eggs and vanilla, beat until fluffy. Combine dry ingredients; add to creamed mixture. Stir in nuts, if desired. Spread in a greased jelly-roll pan. Bake at 350º for 15-18 minutes. Sprinkle marshmallows evenly over cake; return to oven for 2-3 minutes. Using a knife dipped in water, spread the melted marshmallows over cake. Cool. For topping: Combine chocolate chips, butter and peanut butter in a small saucepan. Cook over low heat, stirring constantly until melted and well blended. Remove from heat; stir in cereal; spread over bars. Chill; then cut in squares.
Yield: About 3 doz..

CREAM FILLING FOR CUPCAKES

1 - 8 oz. cream cheese
1/2 c. sugar
1/2 c. nuts

1 egg
1/2 c. coconut
1 c. chocolate chips

Use your favorite chocolate cake recipe or mix. Fill cupcake liners as usual. Mix together filling and add 1 tsp. in each cupcake and bake as usual. Bake at 350º.
Yield: 2 doz.
Paul & Rhonda Borkholder

DOUBLE TREAT COOKIES

Whip together:
2 c. Crisco
2 c. white sugar

2 c. brown sugar
4 eggs
2 tsp. vanilla

Mix thoroughly, then mix in:

3 c. crunchy peanut butter
4 c. flour
4 tsp. baking soda

1 tsp. salt
Chocolate chips

Whip together first 5 ingredients then mix in peanut butter. Sift together dry ingredients and gradually mix in. Shape into balls, flatten with glass dipped in sugar. This has a good peanut butter flavor and I don't always add chocolate chips. Suit your own taste.
Yield: 6 doz.
Linda (Willis) Bontrager

EMMA LOU'S BROWNIES

2 c. flour
1 c. cocoa
1/2 tsp. salt
2 tsp. baking powder
1 1/2 c. Wesson oil
3 c. sugar
6 eggs
2 tsp. vanilla
1 c. chopped English walnuts

Sift together first 4 ingredients and set aside. Beat together sugar and eggs. Add oil and vanilla. Mix in dry ingredients with a spoon. Add nuts last. Pour batter in a sheet cake pan. Bake at 350º for 25 min. or until they test done. If you whip batter too much, it will be more like cake. Just stir until well mixed and they're more gooey!
Emma Lou Bontrager

FIVE GALLON CHURCH COOKIES

2 c. melted lard
4 c. brown sugar
4 c. white sugar
8 beaten eggs
4 c. buttermilk (or 2 T vinegar
   in 4 c. milk)
8 tsp. baking powder
Sam & Ruby Miller
4 tsp. baking soda
4 tsp. nutmeg
1 T. lemon
1 tsp. vanilla
Salt
16 c. flour

FUDGE NUT BARS

1 c. butter, softened
2 c. brown sugar
2 eggs
1 tsp. vanilla
2 c. flour
1 tsp. baking soda
2 1/2 c. oatmeal

Cream butter and brown sugar. Add remaining ingredients. Spread on cookie sheet and bake at 350º for 25-30 minutes. While that is baking, make fudge for the top.

2 c. chocolate chips
2 T. butter
2 tsp. vanilla
1 can sweetened condensed milk
1/2 tsp. salt

Heat until chips are melted and spread on batter part as soon as it comes out of the oven. One c. nuts may be added to fudge, if desired.
Raymond & Martha Bontrager

As empty vessels make the loudest sound, so they that have last wisdom are the greatest babblers.

GINGER SNAPS

2/3 c. shortening
1 c. sugar
1 egg
1/4 c. molasses or honey
2 c. sifted flour

1 tsp. baking soda
1 1/4 tsp. ginger
1 tsp. cinnamon
1/2 tsp. salt
1/2 tsp. clove

Cream shortening and sugar. Blend in egg and molasses. Sift remaining ingredients and add to creamed mixture. Shape in balls about 1" big and roll in white sugar. Place on ungreased cookie sheet. Do not flatten balls. Bake at 325º for 15 minutes.
Monroe W. Miller

GRANDMA'S GINGERSNAPS

2 c. molasses
4 c. sugar
2 c. butter and lard
1 c. hot water
18 c. flour
Grandma Emma Miller

3 tsp. ginger
2 tsp. vinegar
3 tsp. baking soda
2 tsp. rounding full baking powder

GRANDMA'S OATMEAL COOKIES

5 lb. brown sugar
2 1/2 lb. melted lard
2 lb. ground-up raisins
2 lb. quick oatmeal
4 c. buttermilk
7 eggs, beaten

3 T. baking soda
1 T. baking powder
Salt
Vanilla
6 lb. flour

I used to help mix and bake these and can still smell the batter as we were mixing them. Grandpa Levi fashioned cookie sheets from galvanized tin to bake them on. Now we have sheets that bake better and faster than those. We would stop in at Grandma's (Levi Catherine) house to see if our shoes were fixed or if she had a note for us, or bring her some buttermilk. Then she would give us some of these good cookies to eat on the way home. None ever tasted better!
Sam & Ruby Miller

I will bless the Lord at all times: His praise shall continually be in my mouth. Psalms 34:1

Pray for us: for we trust we have a good conscience, in all things willing to live honestly. Hebrews 13:18

MOLASSES CRINKLES

1 1/2 c. shortening, melted
1 c. white sugar
1 c. brown sugar
2 eggs
1/2 c. molasses
5 1/2 c. flour
2 tsp. baking soda
2 tsp. baking powder
1 tsp. cinnamon
1 tsp. ginger or 1/2 tsp. clover
1/2 tsp. salt

Cream shortening and sugar together. Add egg and molasses and beat until well blended. Sift flour, salt, soda and spices together and add to creamed mixture and mix well. Chill dough and then shape dough in balls one inch in diameter. These can be rolled out and cut or rolled into balls and dipped in sugar, then pressed down. Place two inches apart on cookie sheet. Bake 350º for 12-15 minutes. Don't bake it too hard.
Yield: 4 doz.
Sam & Ruby Miller   Joni & Emma Sue Miller

MONSTER PEANUT BUTTER COOKIES

4 sticks butter
4 c. brown sugar
4 c. white sugar
4 tsp. vanilla
8 tsp. baking soda
7 c. pastry flour
12 eggs
6 c. peanut butter (3 lb.)
4 tsp. light Karo
4 c. quick oatmeal
1/4 lb. chocolate chips
1/4 lb. M&M's
2 tsp. salt (optional)

Mix in order given. Drop by spoonful in a pan of flour. Shape into balls, put on cookie sheets and flatten slightly. Bake at 350º for about 12 minutes. Do not overbake! One and a half batches makes a 13 qt. dishpan.
Raymond & Martha Bontrager   Paul & Rhonda Borkholder
        Jacob & Loretta Shetler

OATMEL COOKIES

1 c. hot water
1 c. raisins
2 c. brown sugar
1 c. shortening
4 beaten eggs
4 c. quick oats
1 tsp. baking soda
1 tsp. cinnamon
Vanilla
Salt
2 tsp. baking powder
3 c. flour

1 T. gluten (as a crumb binder - helps keep moist when baked)
Cook raisins in the hot water. Cream together the sugar and shortening and add the rest as a mixture.
Sam & Ruby Miller

OATMEAL SANDWICH COOKIES

4 c. brown sugar
2 1/4 c. butter
6 eggs
3 tsp. vanilla
1 1/2 tsp. salt
3 c. flour
2 1/2 tsp. baking soda

3 tsp. cinnamon
6 c. quick oatmeal
Filling:
3 beaten egg whites
1 c. Crisco
3 c. powdered sugar
1 1/2 tsp. vanilla

Mix ingredients in order given. Drop by teaspoon and flatten a little. Bake at 375°. For the filling, mix all ingredients well. Spread this on one cookie and put another cookie on top.
Ella E. Miller

OLD FASHIONED MOLASSES COOKIES

4 c. molasses
1 c. white sugar
1 c. cold water
1 T. vanilla
1 tsp. salt

3 eggs
2 tsp. baking soda
2 tsp. baking powder
1 tsp. cinnamon
1 tsp. ginger

Add flour to roll or drop on cookie sheets
Add first six ingredients and beat well. If molasses is thin, add 2 c. more for a good flavor. Beat eggs and mix. Now add three or four c. flour with sifter and add the baking powder and baking soda, ginger and cinnamon to the flour. Sift all the flour as needed. The more you use this recipe, the more you'll like it, and the more you'll get the hang of it.
Yield:
Alva & Katie Ann Bontrager

OATMEAL MOLASSES COOKIES

1 c. butter
2 c. baking sorghum molasses
2 eggs
2 1/2 c. whole wheat flour
4 tsp. baking powder
4 tsp. baking soda

1/2 tsp. salt
2 tsp. cinnamon
1 tsp. nutmeg
5 c. quick oatmeal
1 1/2 c. raisins

Melt the butter and molasses together and add the eggs. Sift and mix the dry ingredients together and add that to the mixture. Drop by teaspoons on cookie sheets and bake in a moderate oven until done.
Urie & Lizzie Ann Miller

A true friend is one who knows you're a good egg. . . even if you're slightly cracked!

PEANUT BUTTER CHIP COOKIES

1 c. peanut butter
1 c. butter
3/4 c. sugar
3/4 c. brown sugar
2 eggs

1 c. all-purpose flour
1 c. whole wheat flour
1 tsp. baking soda
1/2 c. chocolate chips

Cream peanut butter and butter in large bowl. Gradually beat in sugar, brown sugar and eggs. Combine all-purpose flour, whole wheat flour and baking soda. Stir into creamed mixture. Add chocolate chips. Drop by spoonfuls on cookie sheet. Flatten with fork. Bake at 350º for 10 minutes.
Yield: 4 doz.
Delilah Stoll

PUMPKIN WHOOPIE PIES

2 egg yolks
2 c. brown sugar
1 c. vegetable oil
2 c. cooked pumpkin
1 tsp. baking powder
1 tsp. baking soda
1 tsp. salt
1 tsp. vanilla
1 tsp. cinnamon
1/2 tsp. cloves

1/2 tsp. ginger
3 c. flour
Filling:
2 unbeaten egg whites
2 T. milk
1 lb. powdered sugar
1 tsp. vanilla
1 c. Crisco
Pinch of salt

Beat together egg yolks, sugar and oil until smooth. Combine remaining ingredients. Drop by teaspoon and flatten. Bake at 350º for 12 minutes. For the filling, mix ingredients together and spread on a cookie. Put another cookie on top - sandwich style.
Wilma M. Miller

PUMPKIN COOKIES

1 c. brown sugar
1/2 c. white sugar
1 c. butter
1 egg
1 tsp. vanilla
1 tsp. baking soda

1 tsp. cinnamon
1 tsp. salt
2 c. flour
1 c. quick or regular oatmeal
1 c. solid pack pumpkin

1 c. chocolate chips or peanut butter chips or raisins
Cream sugars and butter. Add egg and vanilla. Add alternately the dry ingredients and the pumpkin. Bake in 375º oven until firm and slightly brown.
Yield: Approx. 30 cookies

RHUBARB DREAM BARS

Crust:
2 c. flour

3/4 c. powdered sugar
1 c. butter

Filling:

4 eggs, beaten
2 c. sugar
1/2 c. flour

1/2 tsp. salt
4 c. diced rhubarb

Combine flour and sugar; cut in butter until crumbs form. Press onto bottom of cookie sheet. Bake at 350º for 15 minutes. While crust is baking, prepare filling. Blend eggs, sugar, flour and salt until smooth. Fold in rhubarb. Spread over hot crust. Put in oven again and bake at 350º for 40-45 minutes, until filling is lightly browned.
Raymond & Martha Bontrager

SOFT MOLASSES COOKIES

1 c. Crisco
1 1/2 c. sugar
1/2 c. molasses
2 eggs, lightly beaten
4 c. flour

1/2 tsp. salt
2 1/4 tsp. baking soda
2 tsp. ginger
1 tsp. cloves
1 tsp. cinnamon

Cream sugar and shortening together until light and fluffy. Beat in molasses and eggs, set mixture aside. In another bowl, mix dry ingredients with wire whip. Gradually mix flour mix into creamed mix until dough is blended and smooth. Roll dough in 1 1/2" balls, dip tops in granulated sugar, place 2 1/2" apart on greased cookie sheet. Bake at 350º for 11 min. Do not over bake. Store in a tight covered container.
Yield: 3 doz.
Linda (Willis) Bontrager

SORGHUM COOKIES

1/2 gal. sorghum
1 qt. butter or lard
1 c. sugar
1 c. buttermilk
1/2 c. baking soda, scant
1 T. salt

2 T. cinnamon
2 T. nutmeg
25 c. whole wheat flour (5 lb. + 4 c.)
1 qt. chopped nuts
2 lbs. raisins

Roll the dough in balls and flatten on cookie sheets. Bake at 325º-350º until they flatten and are nice and brown, but not burnt. The older they get, the better! Make in October to serve at Christmas.
Yield: 200-300 cookies, depending on size
Urie & Lizzie Ann Miller

The truest end of life is to know the life that never ends.

SOUR CREAM RAISIN BARS

1 c. butter
1 c. brown sugar
2 c. all-purpose flour
2 c. quick-cooking oats
1 tsp. baking powder
1 tsp. baking soda
1/8 tsp. salt

Filling:
4 egg yolks
2 c. or 16 oz. sour cream
1 1/2 c. raisins
1 c. sugar
2 T. cornstarch

In a mixing bowl cream butter and brown sugar. Beat in flour, oats, baking powder, baking soda and salt (mixture will be crumbly). Set aside two cups and pat remaining crumbs into a greased cake pan. Bake at 350º for 15 minutes. Cool. Meanwhile, combine filling ingredients in a saucepan. Bring to a boil; cook and stir constantly for 5-8 minutes. Pour over crust. Sprinkle with reserved crumbs. Return to oven for 15 minutes. A delicious treat! We like them frozen. We double the filling part.
Joni & Emma Sue Miller

SQUASH COOKIES

1 c. lard
2 c. squash/pumpkin (cooked)
2 c. sugar
4 1/2 c. flour, sifted

2 tsp. baking soda
2 tsp. baking powder
2 tsp. cinnamon

Cream together lard, pumpkin, and sugar. Sift in dry ingredients. Add 1 c. nuts, raisins or dates. Frost while still warm. Bake at 350º.
Delilah Stoll

SUGAR COOKIES I

2 T. vinegar
2 c. milk
2 c. shortening, melted
2 c. brown sugar
2 c. white sugar
5 beaten eggs
2 tsp. baking soda

4 tsp. baking powder
8 c. flour
Sour milk
1 T. gluten
1 T. lemon
1 T. vanilla
Salt

Mix the first 3 ingredients and add the rest as a mixture. These are soft moist cookies using Mazola or Blue Bonnet margarine and bread flour.
Sam & Ruby Miller

Always remember to forget The troubles that pass your way
But never forget to remember The blessings that come each day!

SUGAR COOKIES II

5 c. sugar
3 c. lard, melted or vegetable oil
2 1/2 c. sweet milk
1 sm. T. salt
4 eggs

1 T. vanilla
1 tsp. lemon flavor
3 c. flour or more
6 tsp. baking powder
3 tsp. baking soda

In large mixing bowl, beat eggs. Add sugar, oil and vanilla; beat until creamy. Mix dry ingredients. Mix the first four ingredients together. Sift the dry mixture into the bowl. Add enough flour to roll it out. Let this dough set overnight or at least a couple of hours before baking. Bake at 400º. Flour should be added so that dough runs a little when dropped. One way to check the cookie dough is to stick your finger in. If it doesn't hang on your finger, there's enough flour.
Yield: 5 or 6 doz.
Alva & Katie Ann Bontrager   Paul & Rhonda Borkholder

SORGHUM SUGAR COOKIES

2 1/2 c. sugar (use some brown)
1 1/2 c. butter or shortening
2 eggs
4 tsp. baking soda dissolved in
1/2 c. sour cream
1/2 c. sorghum

Mix ingredients in the order given, sifting the dry ingredients together. This will make stiff dough. Chill and then roll in balls the size of a walnut. Dip the tops in sugar and flatten slightly on a cookie sheet. Bake at 350º for 10-15 minutes.
Urie & Lizzie Ann Miller

WORLD'S BEST SUGAR COOKIES

1 c. powder sugar
1 c. white sugar
1 c. margarine
2 eggs
1 tsp. cream of tartar

1 T. salt, scant
1 T. baking soda, scant
5 c. New Rinkle flour
2 tsp. vanilla

Cream sugar and margarine until light and fluffy, then beat in eggs, sift dry ingredients together. Add the first mixture to second mixture and mix well. Roll into balls, and press with a glass dipped in sugar. Bake at 350º for 15 min. on ungreased cookie sheet.
Yield: 3 doz.
Barbara M. Miller

God gave us memories so that we might have roses in December.

TOLL HOUSE OATMEAL COOKIES

1 1/2 c. sifted flour
1 tsp. baking soda
2 c. oatmeal, regular
1 c. nuts, optional
1 pkg. Toll House chocolate
    or butterscotch chips
1 c. shortening

3/4 c. brown sugar
3/4 c. white sugar
2 eggs, beaten
1 tsp. hot water
1 tsp. vanilla
1 tsp. salt

Mix the first 5 ingredients together well. Mix the rest of the ingredients together and dissolve. Add to the dry mixture and mix well. Drop by teaspoon on a cookie sheet. Bake at 350º for ten to 15 minutes.
Yield: 3 doz.
Amos & Elizabeth Miller

TRIPLE FUDGE BROWNIES

1 pkg. instant chocolate pudding mix
1 pkg. chocolate cake mix
2 c. semi-sweet chocolate chips
Confectioner's sugar

Prepare pudding according to package directions. Whisk in dry cake mix. Stir in chocolate chips. Pour into a greased 9 X 13 baking pan. Bake at 350º for 30-35 minutes or until done.
Paul & Rhonda Borkholder

WHITE CHRISTMAS COOKIES

1 c. Crisco
2 c. sugar
2 eggs
1/2 c. cream, or milk
1 tsp. baking soda

2 tsp. salt
1 T. lemon extract
1 T. vanilla
5 c. flour (approx.)

Cream Crisco and sugar, add eggs and beat well. Add baking soda. Mix in cream, or milk, salt and extracts. Roll very thin and cut in various shapes. Decorate with colored sugar, sprinkles, etc. Moderate oven (350º) about five minutes. To keep any length of time, store in tightly covered container.
Yield:
Oba & Laura Borkholder

Each day brings many blessings, but none as sweet as friendship.

Circumstances are like a feather bed: Comfortable if you are on top but smothering if you are underneath!

YUM YUM BARS

2 c. flour
1/2 c. brown sugar
1/2 c. butter, melted
2 c. brown sugar
2 T. flour, rounded
1/4 tsp. baking powder

1 c. coconut
1/2 c. pecans, chopped
1/2 tsp. vanilla
1/2 tsp. salt
3 eggs, beaten

Cream together the first three ingredients and press firmly in the bottom of a 9 X 13 pan. Mix together the rest of the ingredients and pour on top of the crust mixture. Bake at 325º until golden brown - 30 minutes.
Yield: 15 bars
David & Mary Kauffman

TWINKIES

1 box yellow cake mix
1 box instant vanilla pudding
1 1/2 c. water

4 eggs
1/2 c. vegetable oil

Divide into two 9 X 13 pans. Bake at 350º for 10-15 minutes or when a toothpick is inserted and comes out clean. Put a sheet of wax paper in one cake pan and pour batter into it.
Wayne & Kathryn Miller

TWINKIES FILLING

2 egg whites
1 tsp. vanilla

2 c. powdered sugar
1 1/2 c. Crisco, scant

Beat egg whites until stiff. Add the rest of the ingredients and blend together. Spread onto cooled cake, then top with the second layer of cake.
Yield: 1 cake
Wayne & Kathryn Miller

Most people don't recognize opportunity when it knocks because it comes dressed in overalls and looks like a lot of hard work.
-Thomas Edison

The world is composed of takers and givers. The takers may eat better but the givers sleep better.

APPLE CRUNCH

1 c. whole wheat flour
1 c. quick oatmeal
1 c. brown sugar, or less
1 tsp. cinnamon
1/2 tsp. salt, scant
1/2 c. butter

Filling:
1 c. sugar
2 T. cornstarch
1 c. water
1 tsp. vanilla

Mix the first six ingredients together until crumbly. Press half the crumbs into a 9 baking dish. Cover with four c. diced apples. Cook the filling ingredients until thick and clear. Pour over the apples. Top with the remaining crumbs. Bake at 350º for about one hour. This is good served warm with milk or ice cream.
Urie & Lizzie Ann Miller

APPLE DANISH

Pastry:
3 c. all-purpose flour
1/2 tsp. salt
Filling:
6 c. sliced, peeled apples
1 1/2 c. sugar
Glaze:
1 egg white, lightly beaten
1/2 c. confectioner's sugar

1 c. shortening
1 egg yolk
1/2 c. milk

1/4 c. butter, melted
1 tsp. cinnamon

2-3 tsp. water

In mixing bowl, combine flour and salt, cut in shortening until mixture resembles coarse crumbs. Combine egg yolk and milk; add to flour mixture. Stir just until dough clings together. Divide dough in half on lightly floured surface. Roll half of dough into a 15 X 10 rectangle. Place on a 15 X 10 pan and set aside. In a bowl, toss together filling ingredients. Spoon over the pastry in the pan. Roll out the remaining dough and place on top. Brush with egg white. Bake at 375º for 40 minutes or until golden brown. Cool. Combine confectioner's sugar and enough water to achieve drizzling consistency. Drizzle over warm pastry. Cut into squares. Serve warm or cold.
Yield: 20-24 servings

You can live without music, You can live without books,
But show me the one Who can live without cooks!

You start cutting your wisdom teeth the first time you bite off more than you can chew.

APPLE DUMPLINGS

2 c. water
1 1/2 c. brown sugar
2 c. flour
4 tsp. baking powder
1 egg
3 T. vegetable shortening

Pinch of salt
1/2 c. milk
2-3 apples, finely chopped
1/2 - 1 tsp. cinnamon
Butter

Combine brown sugar and water for the syrup in a small saucepan; bring to a boil. Pour into 9 X 13 baking pan. Set aside. Combine shortening, flour, salt and baking powder; combine egg and milk and add to the flour mixture. Mix well. Roll dough out to 1/4 thickness. Spread with filling ingredients (apples, cinnamon & butter), which have been combined. Roll up like cinnamon rolls. Slice into 8-10 rolls. Carefully lay rolls on top of syrup. Dot each roll with butter. Bake at 375º for 20-30 minutes, or until golden brown. Serve hot or cold with milk, whipped cream or ice cream.
Yield: 8-10 rolls

APPLE PUDDING

1/2 c. sugar
2 T. shortening
1 egg
1 c. flour
1/2 tsp. salt

1 tsp. baking powder
1/2 tsp. baking soda
1/2 c. sour milk or buttermilk
1 1/2 c. diced apples
1/2 tsp. vanilla

Cream shortening and sugar. Add the egg and beat well. Add the baking soda into the sour milk and stir into mixture. Add the sifted dry ingredients. Mix thoroughly and stir in apples. Put into a 9x9 inch pan. Rub together the following mixture and sprinkle crumbs over dough:

6 T. brown sugar
1 1/2 tsp. flour

1/2 tsp. cinnamon
1 1/2 tsp. butter

Bake at 375º for 35-40 minutes.
Menno & Malinda Miller

BEST EVER SALAD

4 c. hot water
2 pkg. lime jello
1 lg. pkg. cream cheese
18 lg. marshmallows

1 can crushed pineapple, drained
1 c. pecans
4 c. whipped cream

Dissolve jello in hot water, along with cream cheese and marshmallows, beat until smooth. When semi-thickened, add nuts, pineapple and whipped cream. Nuts and pineapple may be left out.
Yield: 2 avg. size bowls
Barbara Miller

BLACK RASPBERRY TAPIOCA

Heat 4 qt. water to boiling, then add
2 c. fine pearl tapioca
Cook until clear, then add
2 c. sugar
3/4 black raspberry jello
Stir until dissolved; when cold whip.
2 c. heavy cream and mix with
4 pkg. cream cheese
Add this to the tapioca. Now add a quart of fresh black raspberries.
The big and juicy ones work best!
Linda (Willis) Bontrager

BROWNIE PUDDING

1/2 c. sifted flour
1 tsp. baking powder
1/2 tsp. salt
1/3 c. sugar
1/4 c. milk
1 T. cocoa
1 T. melted shortening
1/2 tsp. vanilla
1/4 c. chopped nuts
1/3 c. brown sugar, packed
2 T. cocoa
3/4 c. boiling water

Sift flour, add baking powder, salt, sugar, 1 T. cocoa. Sift again,
then add milk, shortening, vanilla; mix until smooth. Add nuts and
turn into 1 qt. baking dish. Mix together brown sugar and 2 T.
cocoa, sprinkle over batter. Then pour boiling water over top of
batter. This forms a chocolate sauce in bottom of pan as pudding
bakes. Bake at 350º about 35 min.
Yield: 12-15 servings
Aaron & Irene Miller

BUTTERSCOTCH PUDDING

1 c. brown sugar
6 T. flour
1/4 tsp. salt
2 1/2 c. milk
2 egg yolks, beaten
3 T. butter
1 tsp. vanilla

Measure sugar, flour and salt in heavy pan, mix with part of milk to
make a smooth paste. Then add rest of the milk plus beaten eggs.
Stir constantly until it comes to a boil and thickens. Then stir in
butter and vanilla. Let cool. It will also thicken more as it cools.
Layer with graham crackers in a dish or eat it just so.
Glen & Sue Ellen Borkholder

CHERRY TRIANGLES

2/3 c. milk, scalded
2 T. yeast
1 c. butter

2 1/2 c. flour
4 egg yolks, beaten a little

Cherry pie filling, slightly thicker than pie filling

1/4 c. butter
2 T. cream
1/2 tsp. vanilla

1 1/2 c. icing sugar
Nuts

Cool milk to lukewarm and add yeast. Cut the butter into the flour. Add liquid ingredients and yolks to dry ingredients. Mix thoroughly. Turn out on a floured surface and knead about ten times. Roll out half of the dough to fit on a 11 1/2 x 19 1/2 cookie sheet. Spread cooled filling over dough. Roll out the second portion of dough and fit over the bottom part. Pinch edges together. Allow dough to rise for 15 minutes and bake for 45-55 minutes. Cool and frost. Sprinkle with nuts. Cut in 3 squares, then cut each square diagonally, making triangles.
Yield: 4 doz.
Menno & Malinda Miller

COTTAGE CHEESE SALAD

Stir together 1 box Jello (whatever flavor you prefer), 1 pt. Cottage cheese, 1 pkg. Dream Whip, whipped, or 1 can Milnot. Stir and pour into pan and chill overnight. May add fruit of your choice.
Mabel (DeVon) Miller

CRANBERRY SALAD

2 c. cranberries, ground fine
6 sm. apples, chopped coarse
4-5 oranges, sectioned and separated into bits
Chopped English walnuts
Mix into partially set jello made with 2 boxes raspberry jello, sweetened with 1 c. sugar. I've used other jello, too. A delicious looking fruit salad for the holidays!

CREAM CHEESE TURNOVERS

8 oz. cream cheese, softened
2 c. flour
2 T. cream or milk

1 tsp. sugar
1/2 lb. butter

Mix ingredients together and chill one hour in the freezer. You put pie filling on a cut out circle, or if you have a turnover press, that works great. If you don't have a press, just put the filling on a half of a circle, moisten edges, fold in half and flute or press edges together. You can make a couple air holes if you wish. Bake at 350º for 25 minutes.
Glen & Sue Ellen Borkholder

DATE PUDDING

1/2 c. chopped nuts
1 c. chopped dates
1 c. boiling water
1 tsp. baking soda

1 c. sugar
1 egg, beaten
1 T. butter
1 c. flour

Mix boiling water, dates and baking soda together. Let cool. Mix flour, sugar, egg, and butter. Add to the water, dates and baking soda. Mix and add nuts. Put in a 9 X 13 cake pan. Bake at 350º for 25 minutes. Let cool and cut into small squares. Add Cool Whip.
Yield: 8 c.
Amos & Elizabeth Miller

DESSERT BARS

3 c. whole wheat flour
2 c. quick oats
1 1/2 c. brown sugar, packed

1 tsp. salt
1/2 tsp. baking soda
1 1/4 c. butter

Blend well into crumbs. Pat 3/4 of the mixture into the bottom of a 9 X 13 cake pan. Spread with six c. of your favorite fruit or cream pie filling, well thickened. Sprinkle remaining crumbs evenly on top. Pat gently until smooth. Bake in a moderate oven until nicely browned. Note: When making coconut cream bars, add one c. coconut to crumbs.
Yield: 24 servings
Urie & Lizzie Ann Miller

DIRT PUDDING

1 - 12 oz. chocolate Oreo cookies
1/2 stick butter
1 - 8 oz. cream cheese
1 c. powdered sugar
1 - 12 oz. Cool Whip (or whipped tipping)
1 sm. box instant pudding

Crush the cookies with a potato masher. Save some to spread on top. The rest is spread evenly on the bottom of a 9 X 13 cake pan. Set aside. In a mixing bowl, mix butter and cream cheese until fluffy. Add powdered sugar; mix well. Add pudding, which has been mixed according to directions on the box. Fold in Cool Whip. Spread mixture over cookie crumbs. Sprinkle the crumbs you've set back, on top. Note: A cooked, then cooled, pudding may be used instead of the instant.
Yield: 12-18 servings

JELLO SUPREME

1/2 c. (1 box) lemon Jello
1/2 c. (1 box) orange Jello
2 c. boiling water
1 1/2 c. cold water
1 med. can pineapple, drained
2 doz. sm. marshmallows
1 c. pineapple juice
1/2 c. sugar
1 egg
2 T. flour
1 tsp. butter
1 c. Dream Whip
1/2 c. grated cheese

Dissolve Jello in boiling water. Add cold water and let cool. Add drained pineapple and marshmallows. Pour in a pan. For the topping, cook the pineapple juice, egg, sugar, flour and butter together. Put on top of the Jello mixture. Sprinkle with grated cheese.

Allen & Ruth Bontrager

LIME COTTAGE CHEESE

5 (20) c. hot water
1 1/4 c. (5) lemon Jello
1 1/4 c. (5) lime Jello
1 1/4 (5) T. plain gelatin, dissolved in cold water

Melt together. When cooled and partly set add a mixture of:

2 1/2 c. (10) crushed pineapple
2 1/2 c. (10) cottage cheese
1 1/4 c. (5) salad dressing
2 1/2 (10) c. milk

Stir well and pour in bowls. ( ) = measurements to feed approximately 100 people.
Yield:

Sammie & Kathryn Schrock

Patience is the ability to keep your motor idling, when you feel like stripping the gears.

MARSHMALLOW TOPPING

2 c. white sugar   1 c. water
2 1/2 c. light Karo
Cook to 253º then cool 5 min. Add 7/8 c. egg whites (3/4 c. plus 1 egg white = 7/8 c.) beaten stiff and 1/2 c. Karo. Stir. Vanilla may be added if you wish.
Mabel (DeVon) Miller

MARVEL CREAM CHEESE

Make yogurt. Instead of refrigerating the yogurt once it has formed, pour into a colander with triple thickness of cheesecloth, or an old gauze diaper will do. Allow the whey to drip for one minute, then lift up the four corners of the cheese cloth, tie them together then hang up bag to drip for 6-8 hours. Remove from bag. Add sugar (approx. 1/2 c. for 2 qt. yogurt). Store in refrigerator. One qt. yogurt makes about 6-8 oz. cream cheese.
Delilah Stoll

MOON CAKE

1 c. butter   2 boxes instant vanilla pudding
1 c. water   8 oz. cream cheese
1 c. flour   8 oz. Cool Whip
4 eggs
Boil water and butter. Add flour. Stir until flour is used up. Let cool. Beat in eggs, one at a time. Beat really well. Spread on cookie sheet. Bake 25-30 minutes until light brown. Do not try to flatten out crust after it is baked as it is supposed to be bumpy. Mix together pudding and cream cheese, spread on crust. Cover with Cool Whip. Drizzle with chocolate syrup.
Paul & Rhonda Borkholder

ORANGE BUTTERMILK SALAD

1 can (20 oz.) crushed pineapple, undrained
1 pkg. (6 oz.) orange gelatin
2 c. buttermilk
1 carton (8 oz.) frozen whipped topping, thawed
In a saucepan, bring the pineapple to a boil. Remove from the heat; add gelatin and stir to dissolve. Add buttermilk and mix well. Cool to room temperature. Fold in whipped topping. Pour into an 11x7x2 dish. Refrigerate several hours or overnight. Cut into squares.
Yield: 12 servings
Neal & Emma Yoder

PINEAPPLE RICE WHIP

1 - 3 oz. box Jello
3/4 c. boiling water
1 can crushed pineapple, drained

1 3/4 c. cooked rice, cooled
1 c. heavy cream, whipped

Dissolve Jello in boiling water, measure juice, add enough water to make 1 1/4 c.. Add to the dissolved Jello. Refrigerate until set. When Jello is set, whip until foamy and light in color. Add sugar, rice and drained pineapple. Before serving, fold in whipped cream.
Menno & Malinda Miller

PUMPKIN DESSERT

1/2 c. margarine, softened
1 c. flour
1 c. chopped pecans
1 - 14 oz. can sweetened condensed milk
2 c. canned pumpkin
1 - 6 oz. pkg. vanilla instant pudding mix
1 1/2 tsp. pumpkin pie spice
8 oz. whipped topping

Combine margarine, flour and pecans in bowl; mix well. Spread in 9 X 13 baking dish. Bake at 325° for 20 min. Cool. Combine condensed milk, pumpkin, pudding mix, pumpkin pie spice and half the whipped topping in bowl; mix well. Pour over baked layer. Spread remaining whipped topping over filling. Chill in refrigerator.
Yield: 12 servings
Mabel (DeVon) Miller

PUMPKIN PIE SQUARES

1 c. all purpose flour
1/2 c. quick cooking oats
1/2 c. packed brown sugar
1/2 c. butter or margarine
2 cans (15 oz. each) pumpkin
2 cans (12 oz. each) evaporated milk

4 eggs
1 1/2 c. sugar
2 tsp. cinnamon
1 tsp. ginger
1/2 tsp. cloves
1 tsp. salt

Topping:
1/2 c. packed brown sugar
1/2 c. chopped nuts

2 T. butter, softened

Combine the first four ingredients until crumbly; press into a greased 9 X 13 baking pan. Bake at 350° for 20 minutes or until golden brown. Meanwhile, beat the filling ingredients in a mixing bowl until smooth; pour over crust. Bake for 45 minutes. Combine brown sugar, pecans and butter, sprinkle over the top. Bake 15-20 minutes longer or until a knife inserted near the center comes out clean. Cool; store in refrigerator.
Yield: 16-20 servings
Neal & Emma Yoder

RHUBARB CRUNCH

1 c. sugar
1 c. water
2 T. cornstarch
1 tsp. vanilla
1 c. flour

3/4 c. oatmeal
1 c. brown sugar
1/2 c. butter
1 tsp. Cinnamon
4 c. rhubarb

Use the first 4 ingredients to make the syrup. Put rhubarb on bottom of 9 x 9 pan. Pour syrup over rhubarb. Put crunch on top of this. Bake at 350º for 1 hour. This is also good with apples.
Paul & Rhonda Borkholder

RHUBARB SAUCE

10 c. rhubarb
8 c. water

1 c. minute tapioca
3 c. sugar

1 c. Jello (red raspberry, strawberry or cherry)
Cut rhubarb very fine. Put rhubarb and water in a large saucepan. Boil for five minutes. Add tapioca. Stir occasionally. Boil until soft or tapioca looks clear. Add sugar and Jello. Bring to a good boil. Put in jars and give a hot water bath for 5-10 minutes.
Yield: Approx. 4 qt.

RHUBARB TORTE

1 c. flour
2 T. sugar
Pinch of salt
1/2 c. butter
2 1/4 c. rhubarb

1 1/4 c. sugar
1/3 c. top milk
2 T. flour
3 egg yolks

Combine first four ingredients and press into an 8x10 pan and bake at 325º until light brown. In a saucepan, mix the rest of the ingredients. Cook until thick and pour into the baked crust. Top with beaten egg whites, 6 T. sugar and 1/4 tsp. cream of tartar. Brown in 325º oven.
Menno & Malinda Miller

TAPIOCA

2 qt. of boiling water
1 c. pearl tapioca
Pinch of salt
6 oz. of Jello (3/4 c.)

1 c. sugar
Fruit
Cool Whip

Bring water to a boil, add tapioca and salt. Boil for ten minutes. Add Jello and sugar. Let cool. Add fruit and Cool Whip if desired.
Yield: 10 servings
Amos & Elizabeth Miller

THREE LAYER SALAD
boxes Jello (any flavor)
1 - #2 can crushed pineapple (drained)
1/2 c. pecans
1 pkg. cream cheese (8 oz.)
1 c. whitted cream, sweetened to taste
3 eggs
3 T. flour
1 c. sugar
1 c. (or less) pineapple juice
Use the first 3 ingredients for the 1st layer. Use the cream cheese and whitted cream for the 2nd layer. The rest of the ingredients are used for the 3rd layer. Cook 3rd layer until thickened. Cool and spread over 2nd layer.
Yield: 9 X 13 pan
Oba & Laura Borkholder

TRIPLE ORANGE SALAD
1 box orange Jello
1 box instant vanilla pudding
1 box tapioca pudding
2 1/2 c. water
1 c. mandarin oranges
2 c. Cool Whip
Bring Jello, vanilla pudding, tapioca and water to a boil, then take from heat. Cool. Add Cool Whip and mandarin oranges. May substitute strawberry Jello and strawberries.
Mabel (DeVon) Miller

TRIPLE TREAT TORTE
1/2 c. cold butter
1 c. flour
2/3 c. chopped nuts
1 - 8 oz. cream cheese, softened
1/2 c. creamy peanut butter
1 - 8 oz. whipped topping, divided
1 pkg. instant chocolate pudding
1 pkg. instant vanilla pudding
1 c. powdered sugar
2 3/4 c. cold milk
Use the first 3 ingredients for the crust, the next 5 for the filling, and the last 3 for the topping. Cut butter into flour until crumbly; stir in nuts. Press into greased 9x 13 pan. Bake at 350º for 16-20 minutes or until golden brown. Cool completely. Beat powdered sugar, cream cheese and peanut butter until smooth. Fold in 1 c. whipped topping. Spread over crust. In another bowl, combine pudding mixes and milk, beat for 2 minutes. Spread over filling. Top with remaining whipped topping. Cover and refrigerate 4 hours or overnight.
Paul & Rhonda Borkholder

TWELVE LAYER JELLO SALAD

3 oz. pkg. Jello of each flavor: Cherry, Lime, Lemon, Orange, Strawberry
16 oz. sour cream
Add 1 c. boiling water to cherry Jello, take out half and add to 1/3 c. sour cream, slowly. Pour in clear 9 X 13 pan. Chill 20 minutes or until firm. Add 3 T. cold water to remaining Jello and pour on top of first layer. Let set. Repeat the same with each following Jello flavor. Fix Jello in order given and it will look nice in your pan.
Raymond & Martha Bontrager

REFRIGERATOR PUDDING

1/2 c. butter   1 1/2 pkg. graham crackers
Crush graham crackers, melt butter and mix. Press into the bottom of a Tupperware pan, except reserve one c. to sprinkle on top of pudding.
1 c. boiling water   1/3 c. strawberry Jello
    Dissolve Jello in water and cool until slightly jelled.
8 oz. cream cheese   1 c. white sugar
Cream together cream cheese and sugar until fluffy. Whip 2 c. Riches topping until stiff and add 1 tsp. vanilla. Mix together Jello mixture, Riches topping and cream cheese mixture until blended. Pour onto graham cracker crust. Sprinkle remaining crumbs on top and refrigerate. Delicious!
Yield:
Mary J. Miller (Joni)

RIBBON MOLD

2 pkg. (3 oz.) black cherry gelatin
2 pkg. (3 oz.) lemon gelatin
2 pkg. (3 oz.) lime gelatin
2 pkg. (3 oz.) orange gelatin
1 pkg. (3 oz.) strawberry gelatin
1 can (13 oz.) evaporated milk
Add water to evaporated milk to make 16 oz. Dissolve 1 pkg. black cherry gelatin in 1 c. boiling water. Add 1/2 c. cold water. Pour into 9 X 13 pan. Chill until firm. Dissolve second pkg. black cherry gelatin in 1 c. boiling water. Add 1/2 c. evaporated milk. Pour onto first layer. Chill until firm. Continue making clear and creamy layers. End with clear layer of strawberry gelatin. When very firm, unmold and garnish, if desired.
Yield: 24 servings
Wayne & Kathryn Miller

A good spirit attracts friends.

WEDDING FRUIT MIX

1 gal. fruit cocktail
2 gal. peaches
1 gal. pineapple chunks
1 pkg. orange Kool-Aid
6 c. sugar
2 1/2 c. clear jell

Kool-Aid
2 qt. red seedless grapes
2 qt. green grapes
2 qt. apples, unpeeled
12 kiwis
2 qt. fresh strawberries

Drain the fruit and save the juices. Add enough pineapple juice to make 1 1/2 gal.; also add 1/2 qt. of water. Thicken with clear jel, sugar and Kool-Aid. On morning of the wedding, cut grapes in half, chunk apples, slice kiwi crosswise and mix. You can also add oranges, tangerines or bananas. But leftovers can be canned if the bananas are left out.
Yield: Double recipe will serve 200 guests
Sammie & Kathryn Schrock

ZUCCHINI DESSERT SQUARES

4 c. all-purpose flour
2 c. sugar
1/2 tsp. ground cinnamon
Filling:
8-10 c. cubed, seeded, peeled zucchini
1/2 c. Realemon juice

1/2 tsp. salt
1 1/2 c. cold butter

1 c. sugar
1 tsp. cinnamon
1/2 tsp. nutmeg

In a bowl, combine flour, sugar, cinnamon and salt. Cut in the butter until crumbly; reserve three c.. Pat remaining crumb mixture into the bottom of a greased 9 X 13 baking pan. Bake at 375º for 12 minutes. Meanwhile, for filling, place the zucchini and lemon juice in a saucepan and bring to a boil. Reduce heat; cover and cook for 6-8 minutes or until zucchini is crisp-tender. Stir in sugar, cinnamon and nutmeg; cover and simmer for five minutes. (Mixture will be thin.) Spoon over crust. Sprinkle with reserved crumb mixture. Bake at 375(for 40-45 minutes or until golden. This tastes just like apple bars in the middle of summer.
Yield: 16-20 servings

HOMEMADE ICE CREAM I

8 eggs whipped well
1 c. white sugar

1 c. brown sugar

Add a little bit of milk to the mixture. Beat well until sugar is dissolved. Add vanilla to taste. Add 2 small boxes instant pudding, any flavor. Mix well. 1 pt. whipping cream - whip until stiff and add to mixture. Mix well. Add milk for the desired amount to fill your freezer can about 3/4 full or so. Freeze and enjoy an award winning dessert! As they say, "it'll lay you out flat."
DeVon Miller

HOMEMADE ICE CREAM II

2 qt. milk
4 eggs
2 1/2 c. sugar
2 tsp. salt

1 c. flour plus 2 T. cornstarch
2 tsp. vanilla
3/4 c. whipped topping (don't cook)

Put the milk in a six-qt. kettle. Add enough milk to flour, sugar and egg mixture to stir well and add that to the hot milk; cook until thickened. Add vanilla and cool. Pour in 1 1/2 gal. ice cream can. Add enough milk to fill to the second paddle. Sprinkle 3/4 c. whipped topping on top. Freeze. If you have cream, add that instead of the whipped topping and so much milk.
Yield: 1 1/2 gal.

LEMON ICE CREAM

3 eggs
1 tbs. vanilla
11/4 cups sugar

11/2 qt. milk
1 cup cream
1 tbs. lemon flavoring

Beat the eggs until light. Add the sugar and continue beating until smooth. Add the cream and the flavorings and mix thoroughly. Add vanilla and freeze. When the desired consistency, remove the paddle and pack the ice cream in salt and ice mixture. One quart of crushed strawberries (sweetened) may be added to the ice cream if desired or the plain ice cream is delicious served with chocolate sauce.
Yield: 2 quarts

OLD-FASHIONED
STRAWBERRY ICE CREAM

1 cup milk
3 eggs
2 cups heavy cream, whipped
2 cups sugar

1/8 tsp. salt
2 cups crushed berries
I tbs. flour or cornstarch

Scald milk and stir, thoroughly and slowly, into well-beaten eggs, 1 cup of sugar, salt and flour or cornstarch. Cook in double boiler, stirring constantly until mixture thickens. Remove from heat and, when cold, fold in whipped cream. When partially frozen, stir in the strawberries which have been crushed and pressed through a sieve and sweetened with remaining sugar. Freeze.
Yield: 2 quarts

CHOCOLATE ICE CREAM TOPPING

1 c. sugar
1/2 T. cornstarch

1 T. cocoa
Some water

It will be thin. Boil well for 5-6 minutes. Remove from heat and add vanilla.
Ivan & Martha Miller

VELVET ICE CREAM

1 qt. milk
2 tbs. cornstarch
2 cups heavy cream, whipped
2 cups brown sugar
4 egg yolks, beaten
1/2 tsp. maple flavoring
4 egg whites, stiffly beaten
1/4 tsp. salt

Heat the milk to scalding. Mix the sugar with the cornstarch and egg yolks. Gradually add the scalded milk and cook until the mixture begins to thicken, stirring constantly. Remove from stove, add salt and flavoring, and set aside to cool. Fold egg whites and whipped cream into the cooled custard and freeze.
Yield: 2 quarts

HOMEMADE FRIENDLY FLORA YOGURT

1 gal. sweet milk (skimmed)
1 c. yogurt or starter
4 T. plain gelatin (dissolved in cup of cold milk)
1/2 c. Jello or pie filling (any flavor)
1-2 c. sugar (optional)
3 tsp. vanilla (optional)

Pour one gal. milk in a large saucepan. Heat to 180º stirring often then cool to constant heat at 140º. Skim off the milk "hide." Stir in yogurt or starter from store until dissolved. Dip out one c. and save as a starter for the next time. Pour through a strainer.
Add vanilla, sugar and gelatin and Jello or pie filling and stir until dissolved. Put in jars and place near the stove pilot light where it's warm - overnight or at least 8 hours. If oven is not warm enough, wrap it in a towel to keep warm. Cool in refrigerator - but don't freeze. The mixture should then be set. Yogurt is a wonderful lowfat substitute used for salad dressing, cottage cheese or chip dips. Yummy!
Yield: 4 qt.

Jacob & Loretta Shetler   Joni & Emma Sue Miller
Sammie & Kathryn Schrock   Delilah Stoll   Aaron & Irene Miller

BAR-B-Q SAUCE

1 1/2 qt. water
1 3/4 c. vinegar
2 T. garlic salt
2 1/2 T. Worcestershire sauce
1/2 c. salt
1/2 c. sugar
2 T. black pepper
3/4 lb. butter
Baste chicken with this sauce each time you turn it.
Yield:
Joni & Emma Sue Miller

CHEESE BALL

2 - 8 oz. cream cheese
5-6 T. sour cream and onion powder
1/4 c. milk (more or less)
1 pkg. meat, cut fine
Mix cream cheese, sour cream and onion powder and milk. Then add meat. Chill. Roll in pecan pieces and serve with crackers. Add cheddar cheese powder if you want a cheddar cheese ball.
Yield: 2 balls
Paul & Rhonda Borkholder

CHIP OR CRACKER DIP

1 - 8 oz. pkg. cream cheese
1 can any cheese
1 T. Worcestershire sauce
1/4 tsp. garlic flakes or salt
1 tsp. onion flakes or salt
1 pkg. dried beef or bacon bits
Mix together. Better when set for a couple of hours.
Barbara Miller

COLE SLAW DRESSING

For 1 medium head of cabbage:

3/4 c. sugar
1 c. salad dressing
2 T. vinegar
1 tsp. prepared mustard
1/2 tsp. celery seed
1 tsp. salt

For 3 gal. shredded cabbage:

3 c. sugar
1 qt. salad dressing
8 T. vinegar
4 tsp. mustard
2 tsp. celery seed
4 tsp. salt

Cole slaw will keep well in the refrigerator for up to a few days with this dressing.
Urie & Lizzie Ann Miller

HAMBURGER AND BEAN SAUCE
1 qt. frozen or canned hamburger
1 onion
1 qt. chunky pizza sauce
1 can kidney beans (may substitute)
Mushrooms, optional
Take cast iron skillet and brown hamburger and onion. Then add pizza sauce and beans. Let simmer for 15 min. We like to eat this with cornbread or add mozzarella cheese on top and melt, then eat with tortilla chips. This is quick and easy - especially if you have cornbread made ahead.
Linda (Willis) Bontrager

KETCHUP
1 gal. thick tomato juice
1 tsp. cayenne pepper
2 1/3 c. sugar
1 1/2 onions, put in blender or
1 1/2 tsp. onion salt

Bring to a brisk boil and simmer briskly until half volume. Add to:
1 1/4 c. vinegar
2 tsp. celery seed
1 tsp. mustard seed
1 tsp. cinnamon
1 tsp. paprika
1 tsp. mixed pickling spices

ORANGE FRUIT DIP
1 pkg. 8 oz. cream cheese
1 c. marshmallow creme
Grated peel of one orange

Combine all ingredients and mix well. Serve with fresh fruits.
Yield:
Virgil & Esther Yoder

MIRACLE WHIP
1/2 c. Clear Jell
1 1/2 c. water
1/2 c. vinegar
1/3 - 2/3 c. sugar
2 tsp. salt
3/4 c. vegetable oil
1 T. lemon juice
1/2 tsp. dry mustard
1/2 tsp. garlic powder or salt
1/2 tsp. onion salt or powder

1 egg plus water to make 3/4 c.
Cook the first five ingredients together. Beat the remaining ingredients in a bowl and combine with the first mixture. This makes one qt. We make two batches of this and add one qt. of store-bought salad dressing to it. It's hard to tell the difference.
Yield:

There is so much good in the worst of us, and so much bad in the best of us, that it hardly behooves any of us to talk about the rest of us.

OUR FAVORITE KETCHUP

2 1/2 gal. tomatoes, mashed (use small or Roma tomatoes)
4 tsp. salt
2 c. sugar
2 c. vinegar
2 1/2 c. Perma Flo, mixed with water to right consistency
Cook tomatoes with four medium onions and 2 1/2 T. pickling spice. Put through the strainer. (If using a Victorio strainer, tie the pickling spice into a cloth bag.) Use two kettles. Put a gal. of juice in each kettle. Add the salt, sugar and vinegar. Cook for 30 minutes. Add half of the Perma Flo in each kettle. Stir until thick and bubbly. Add one gal. of Hunt's ketchup (optional). Put in jars and seal.
Yield: 24 pt.
Monroe & Elsie Miller

PIZZA DIP

1 - 8 oz. cream cheese   1/2 c. sour cream
1 tsp. oregano   1/8 tsp. garlic powder
1/8 tsp. red pepper
Mix together and put in bottom of 9" pan.
Next, layer the following:
1/2 c. pizza sauce
1/2 c. pepperoni, chopped fine
1/2 c. green pepper, chopped fine
1/2 c. chopped onions
1/2 c. shredded mozzarella cheese
Bake for 10 minutes at 350º, then put cheese on top and bake 5 minutes longer. Serve warm with crackers or chips.
Yield:
Virgil & Esther Yoder   Paul & Rhonda Borkholder

RUBY'S CHILI SAUCE

30 ripe tomatoes   2 T. salt
6-8 onions, chopped   Sm. bag of whole spices:
1 bunch celery, chopped   1 T. ground allspice
2 green peppers   1 tsp. ginger
2 c. white sugar   1 tsp. celery seed
1 c. brown sugar   1 tsp. cinnamon
3 c. white vinegar   1 tsp. nutmeg
Put tomatoes through the Victorio strainer. Mix in all the rest of the ingredients. Cook in an oven at 325º for 4-5 hours. I use a roasting pan, uncovered.
Menno & Malinda Miller

SALSA

6 hot peppers (with seeds)	14 lbs. tomatoes
10 green sweet peppers	2 1/2 lbs. onions
Make a gravy with:	
1 c. vinegar	2 T. chili powder
1/4 c. sugar	2 T. oregano
1/4 c. salt	1 c. Perma-Flo
1 1/2 T. garlic powder	Liquid hot sauce to taste

Chop vegetables fine or put through salsa master. Cook in a large kettle until tender; about 10 minutes. Add the spicy gravy mixture and bring to a boil. Ladle into jars and cold pack 10 minutes in boiling water bath.
Yield: 18 pt.
Oba & Laura Borkholder

TOMATO PULP

Cook down to 1/3, or less, of total amount with a bag of 2 T. mixed pickling spices tied in. Mix dry ingredients and have ready to thicken pulp when cooked down.

6 T. salt	1 tsp. cloves
2 tsp. cinnamon	4 c. brown sugar
2 tsp. allspice	5 c. white sugar
2 tsp. dry mustard	5 heaping T. clear jell
2 tsp. paprika	

Mix well and add 1 qt. vinegar. Beat and pour into ketchup bottles and seal.
Delilah Stoll

TARTAR SAUCE

12 lg. green tomatoes	3 c. sugar
12 sm. green peppers	4 tsp. salt
4 med. onions	1/2 c. flour
1 c. prepared mustard	1 qt. salad dressing
1 c. vinegar	

Grind tomatoes, peppers and onions together and drain. Pour enough boiling water over this to cover completely. Let set for two minutes; then bring to a boil. Add the rest of the ingredients. Boil for 15 minutes. Add thickening of water and 1/2 c. flour. Boil another ten minutes. Add salad dressing while hot. Stir well and put in jars and seal.
Yield: 10-12 pt.
Sammie & Kathryn Schrock

WESTERN BARBEQUE SAUCE

1/2 c. ketchup
1/3 c. vinegar
1/4 c. Worcestershire sauce
2 T. brown sugar
2 tsp. chili powder

Lemon juice
1/2 tsp. dry mustard
1/2 tsp. garlic salt
1/2 tsp. onion powder
1/4 tsp. cayenne pepper

Brush on hamburgers when almost done. Also good on fried chicken.
Yield:
Joni & Emma Sue Miller

BAR-B-Q SEASONED FLOUR

1 c. flour
2 tsp. pepper
6 tsp. salt

4 tsp. paprika
2 tsp. dry mustard

Mix all ingredients and keep in a tight container ready to use. For quick, I add 2 T. Lawry's seasoning to 2 c. flour, if on hand. This is a standard coating for chicken, beef, zucchini, fish or whatever. Whatever you use it on should be drained, patted dry, then coated with oil or milk or beaten eggs, so the flour will stick. Use for baking or frying. Delicious! Very good!
Yield: About 2 c.
Sam & Ruby Miller   Sammie & Kathryn Schrock   Delilah Stoll

BAR-B-Q SEASON FLOUR FOR CHICKEN

Small batch:
1/2 c. flour
1 tsp. pepper
3 tsp. salt
2 tsp. paprika
1/4 tsp. dry mustard

Large batch: (x8)
4 c. flour
8 tsp. pepper
1/3 c. salt
1/2 c. paprika
4 tsp. dry mustard

Mix and keep in a tight container ready to use. For quick, I add 2 T. Lawry's seasoning to 2 c. flour, if on hand.
Delilah Stoll

STROH'S SEASONED FLOUR

4 tsp. seasoned salt
2 tsp. paprika
1 tsp. salt

1 tsp. sage
1 tsp. cayenne pepper
3 c. flour

This be used on meats and fried green tomatoes, zucchini, etc. Dip in oil, beaten egg or milk, before dipping in this flour coating.
Sam & Ruby Miller

FINGER JELLO

1/3 c. Knox gelatin
2 c. cold water
1 c. Jello (2 pkg.)
1/4 c. sugar
2 1/2 c. boiling water

Dissolve gelatin in the cold water. Add the gelatin to the other ingredients, stirring until everything is dissolved. Add one c. of cold water. Pour into a cake pan and let set.
Jacob & Loretta Shetler

FRENCH FRIED ONION RINGS

1 c. pancake mix
1 egg
1 T. Wesson oil
1/2 c. boiling water
1/2 tsp. chicken base
Oil to fry

Mix all together. Dip onion rings in and fry in oil, heated to 350º.
Mabel (DeVon) Miller

GRAHAM CRACKERS

2 c. brown sugar
1 tsp. soda
1 tsp. salt
1 tsp. vanilla
2 c. flour
1 c. shortening
1 tsp. baking powder
1 c. milk

Roll thin; cut and prick with fork. Bake in 350º oven until nice and brown.
Mabel (DeVon) Miller

HAM ROLL UPS

1 1/2 stick butter
2 - 8 oz. cream cheese
1 pkg. cheddar cheese

Mix together and spread on ham. Roll up and slice after chilled.
Mabel (DeVon) Miller

MONKEY BREAD

3 cans biscuits (10 to a can)
3/4 c. sugar
1 1/2 tsp. cinnamon
1/2 c. nuts (optional)
3/4 c. butter
1 c. sugar
1 1/4 tsp. cinnamon

Cut each biscuit into 4 pieces and shake in a mixture of sugar and cinnamon. Drop into bundt pan. Sprinkle with nuts. In a small saucepan, combine topping ingredients (last 3 ingredients) and bring to a boil. Pour over biscuits and bake at 350º for 40-45 minutes. Turn out on a plate and enjoy.
Paul & Rhonda Borkholder

PARTY MIX

2 1/2 sticks butter
3 T. Worcestershire sauce
1/2 tsp. garlic powder

3/4 tsp. celery salt
2 1/2 tsp. vega-salt
35 c. cereal, pretzels, etc.

Melt together and pour over 35 c. of cereal such as Chex, pretzels, Cheerios, Cheese Nips, Crispix or whatever you desire. Take 1/2 pkg. Hidden Valley Ranch powder and sprinkle over mix. Mix well. Bake at 250º for 1 hour, stirring every 15 minutes.
Raymond & Martha Bontrager

PECAN SQUARES

3 c. flour
1/2 c. sugar

1 c. butter, softened
1/2 tsp. salt

In large mixing bowl, blend together flour, sugar, butter and salt until mixture resembles coarse crumbs. Press firmly and evenly into a greased 15 X 10x1 baking pan. Bake at 350º for 20 minutes.

4 eggs

1 1/2 c. light or dark corn syrup
1 1/2 c. sugar

3 T. butter, melted
1 1/2 tsp. vanilla
2 1/2 c. chopped pecans

In another bowl, combine first 5 filling ingredients. Stir in pecans. Spread evenly over hot crust. Bake at 350º for 25 minutes or until set.
Paul & Rhonda Borkholder

TORTILLA ROLL UPS

1 pkg. cream cheese
1 tsp. Lawry's
2 T. Worcestershire sauce
1/4 lb. shaved ham, cut fine

1 tsp. minced onion
A little liquid smoke
Flour tortilla shells

Mix the first 6 ingredients well and spread on flour tortillas. Roll up and cut in 3/4" lengths and insert toothpick. Some add fine chopped jalapeno peppers too. This goes good on a relish tray, etc.
Linda (Willis) Bontrager

OYSTER CRACKER SNACK

1 box (approx. 14 oz.) oyster crackers
1 pkg. ranch mix (dry)

A little Italian mix
1/2 c. of cooking oil

Mix all together in a large mixing bowl. Ready to eat!
Glen & Sue Ellen Borkholder

Kindness is a language which the deaf man can hear and the blind man read.

CINNAMON CANDY POPCORN

8 qt. plain popped popcorn   1/2 c. light corn syrup
1 c. butter or margarine   1 pkg. (9 oz.) red-hot candies

Place popcorn in a large bowl and set aside. In a saucepan, combine butter, corn syrup and candies; bring to a boil over medium heat, stirring constantly. Boil for five minutes, stirring occasionally. Pour over popcorn and mix thoroughly. Turn into two greased 15 X 10x1 baking pans. Bake at 250º for one hour, stirring every 15 minutes. Remove from pans and cool. Break apart, store in air tight containers or plastic bags.
Yield: 8 qt.
Neal & Emma Yoder

PARTY MIX

2 - 10 oz. boxes oyster crackers   2 - 2 oz. pkg. Hidden Valley
1/2 c. warm salad oil   Ranch Mix
Add the following to the oil: 1/2 tsp. dill weed
                                  1/4 tsp. lemon pepper

Pour over crackers and mix, mix, mix. Put in zip lock bags.
Sam & Ruby Miller

SOFT PRETZELS

2 c. thesco (bread) flour   1 1/2 c. lukewarm water
2 c. regular flour   1 scant tsp. salt
1/4 c. brown sugar   2 tsp. yeast

Second recipe variation: 4 1/2 c. regular flour; 1 T. brown sugar; 1 3/4 c. lukewarm water; 1 tsp. salt; 2 T. yeast; 2 tsp. baking soda. Dissolve yeast in brown sugar and water. Mix all ingredients together thoroughly. Let rise for 15 minutes. Shape into 10 pretzels. Dip each pretzel into a solution of 2 c. warm water and 1 T. baking soda. Place the pretzels on a well greased cookie sheet and sprinkle with salt. Bake for 5-10 minutes at 500º. Dip into melted butter. Very simple and delicious!
Yield: 10 pretzels
Glen & Sue Ellen Borkholder

SWEET SNACK MIX

14 c. popped popcorn   1 lb. white confectioner's coating
3 c. crisp rice cereal   3 T. creamy peanut butter
2 c. salted peanuts

In a bowl combine popcorn, cereal and peanuts. In the top of a double boiler over simmering water, melt the coating and peanut butter, stirring occasionally. Pour over the popcorn mixture and stir to coat. Spread evenly on waxed paper and allow to set. Store in an airtight container.
Yield: 5-6 qt.
Neal & Emma Yoder

On Your Wedding Day

FAMILY GAME

On slips of paper write the four members of each family that you choose, such as Farmer, Farmer's Wife, Farmer's Daughter, Farmer's Son; Carpenter, Carpenter's Wife, Carpenter's Daughter, Carpenter's Son; Doctor, Dentist, etc., until you have 20 sets more or less, depending on the number of players. Turn slips face down on table and mix up. Each player draws four slips. Keep slips inside cover of a book or magazine so players can't see those of each other. Each player takes turns asking another player for a member only out of a family you already have one of. If they have it, it is handed to the person requesting it. Listen carefully, and you will be able to figure out where the family members lie. Every time you complete a turn, you pick up another slip from the pile. Every time you request a correct family member, you take another turn. It's similar to a memory game.

Urie & Lizzie Miller

MARBLE GAME BOARD - GAME FOR 2

Make a board with 12 holes, five on each side and one on each end. Using 50 marbles, put five marbles into each side hole. The two end holes are home base for each player. How to play: The first player takes all the marbles from any of his slots and drops one marble in each of the following slots going counter-clockwise. If the last marble is dropped into home base, he may have another turn. The object of the game is to have your five slots empty first. Any marbles in home base are not to be removed during the game and are safe. This is a very simple yet challenging game for young and old alike.

Jacob Shetler

PLAY DOUGH

2 c. pastry flour
1/2 c. cornstarch
1 c. salt

1 T. salad or cooking oil
2 c. water
Food coloring

1 T. powdered alum or 1/2 - 2 tsp. cream of tartar

Mix first four ingredients in a three qt. kettle. Add oil and water and coloring. Stir to make a smooth paste. Put on low heat, stir constantly until mixture thickens to dough consistency. Let cool and then knead like bread for a few minutes until smooth. Our children play for hours using a table knife, rolling pin, cookie cutters, letter cut-outs to spell their names, and small pie pans to make their own little pies. Keep in an airtight container or plastic bag. Stays nice for a long time. This is safe and non-toxic.

Joni & Emma Sue Miller   Allen & Ruth Bontrager
Raymond & Martha Bontrager Monroe & Elsie Miller Delilah Stoll

GIANT BLOWING BUBBLES
1 c. liquid detergent, a good kind
4 oz. Glycerin
1/2 gal. Water
1 T sugar
Mix together. Use a plastic pop can holder or a wire twisted in a circle.

SANDBOX FUN
A sandbox has many creations for the tiny tots. They even plant "fields" of real oats and barley to see it grow! Also have a "shed" of half a hollow log we found when making wood.
Delilah Stoll

STILTS
These "extended legs" will bring some laughs. For a grown person, take two 2 X 4's anywhere from 5'-8' long (any length) and slender down one end of each so they may be gripped comfortably with the hands. Cut two pieces of 2 X 4 about 6"-8" long for steps. Fasten the _ends_ of these against the sides of the long pieces about 3'-4' down from the top. Use 2 strips of nylon or leather scraps as a brace for the steps. Fasten one end to the side of the long piece about a foot above the step and the other end of the brace gets fastened to the end of the step which points away from the long piece. After completing the stilts, we used to back up against a building, step up on the steps, hold the top ends under our arms close to our bodies, and walk away. Besides being able to "look down our noses at others," we enjoyed the scenery from a different "viewpoint." Happy stilting!
DeVon Miller

WAGON WHEELS
Remember the treasures we found scavenging trash piles? One thing we used to look for were little wagon wheels. We took a flat stick about 3' long and fastened a 6"-8" cross piece at the bottom end. We would then start our wheel rolling and "chase" it around and around with our "cross." If we became good at it, we could even make short turns. We used to run and run, chasing our wheels around.
DeVon Miller

Put a brown paper bag or a cup of corn starch inside the refrigerator to remove strong odors

Thinking of you

Happy,

Birthday,

AMAZING CLEANSER

1 c. ammonia
1/2 c. vinegar

1/4 c. baking soda
1 gal. water

This is for cleaning walls and taking wax off floors.
Sammie & Kathryn Schrock

ANT REPELLENT

Spray 50% white distilled vinegar on counter tops, window sills and shelves and wipe, leaving residue. Start early in spring before they arrive, because it takes a few weeks to rid yourself of them once they are established. If you want immediate action, get some lemons, cut the yellow outer peel off and cover with grain alcohol in a tightly closed jar. Let stand at least one hour. Use 1 part of this concentrate with 9 parts water in a spray bottle. Mix only as much as you will use because the diluted form loses potency. Spray walls, floors, carpets wherever you see them. The lemon solution even leaves a shine on your counters. Use both vinegar and lemon approaches to rid yourself of ants.
To treat the whole house, pour vinegar all around your foundation, close to the wall, using one gallon for every five feet. Expect to damage any foliage it touches. Reapply every six months.

BABY WIPES

2 c. boiling water
3 T. baby bath

1 T. baby oil

Cut one roll of Bounty paper towels in half. Remove center cardboard. Place upright in airtight container and pour solution over it. Cover tightly and it's ready to use in one hour. The wipes can be pulled up from the center just like store-bought ones, and torn off at any length. This is a quick and easy recipe, plus a real time saver.
Mabel (DeVon) Miller   Sammie & Kathryn Schrock

BLIGHT SPRAY

1 bar Ivory soap
4 oz. salt petre
4 oz. Borax

3 qt. rain water
1 pt. household ammonia

Dissolve the bar soap in one qt. of warm water. Be sure not to get too hot. Add the rest of the ingredients and mix well. Store in a glass jar for a few months before using. This will keep for years. To use: Mix one T. of mixture to one qt. of water to spray plants. If blight is bad, spray twice a week. Use as soon as the first signs of blight appears. Use on vegetables and melons. When

tomatoes are done blooming, spray once a week, but not before a rain.
Yield: 1 gal.
Neal & Emma Yoder

BRUSHING TEETH

Buy a new toothbrush. Your old one is soaked with toxins from your old toothpaste. Use only water or chemically pure baking soda if you have any metal fillings. Put a pinch in a glass, add water to dissolve it. Use good-grade hydrogen peroxide if you have only plastic fillings. Dilute it from 35% to 17 1/2% by adding water (equal parts). Store hydrogen peroxide only in polyethylene or the original plastic bottle. Use 4 or 5 drops on your toothbrush. It should fizz nicely as oxygen is produced in your mouth. Your teeth will whiten noticeably in 6 months. Before brushing teeth, floss with 4 or 2 lb. monofilament fish line. Double it and twist for extra strength. Rinse before use. Floss and brush only once a day. If this leaves you uncomfortable, brush the extra times with plain water and a second "water-only" toothbrush. Make sure that nothing solid, like powder, is on your toothbrush; it will scour the enamel and give you sensitive teeth, especially as you get older and the enamel softens. Salt is corrosive - don't use it for brushing metal teeth. Plain water is just as good.

BORAX LIQUID SOAP

Empty 1 gal. jug   Plastic funnel
1/8 c. Borax powder
Funnel the Borax into the jug, fill with cold tap water. Shake a few times. Let settle. In a few minutes you can pour off the clear part into dispenser bottles. This is the soap!
Easier way: use any bottle, pour Borax powder to a depth of an 1/2" or so. Add water. Shake. When you have used it down to the undissolved granules, add more water and shake again. Add more Borax when the undissolved granules get low.
Keep a dispenser by the kitchen sink, bathroom sink, and shower. It does not contain aluminum as regular detergents and soaps do, and which probably contribute to Alzheimer's disease. It does not contain PCBs as many commercial and health food varieties do. It does not contain cobalt (the blue or green granules) which causes heart disease and draws cancer parasites to the skin. Commercial detergents and non-soaps are simply not safe. Switch to homemade bar soap and Borax for all your tasks! Borax inhibits the bacterial enzyme urease and is therefore antibacterial. It may even clear your skin of blemishes and stop your scalp from itching.

102

CARPET CLEANER

Whether you rent a machine or have a cleaning service, don't use the carpet shampoo they want to sell, even if they "guarantee" that it is all natural and safe. Instead add these to a bucket (about 4 gal.) of water and use it as the cleaning solution:

Wash Water
1/3 c. Borax
Rinse Water
1/4 c. grain alcohol
2 tsp. boric acid

1/4 c. white distilled vinegar
or
4 tsp. citric acid

Borax does the cleaning; alcohol disinfects, boric acid leaves a pesticide residue, and the vinegar or citric acid give luster. If you are just making one pass on your carpet, use the borax, alcohol, and boric acid. Remember to test everything you use on an unnoticed piece of carpet first.

COLD SOAP FOR LAUNDRY

5 pt. cold water
2 cans lye
4 T. white sugar
4 T. ammonia
1/2 c. Sal soda

1/2 c. Borax
2 oz. glycerin
1 oz. oil of sassafras
1 box Tide

Use a granite or iron kettle and combine all of the above ingredients. Let come to right temperature (lukewarm) and stir until everything has dissolved. Then pour this mixture into 10 lbs. of melted lard. (Never pour the lard into lye.) Stir oft about 20 minutes until creamy. Let it harden then cut into pieces before it gets too hard. When partly dried, press through 1/4 inch hardware mesh. Put soap in cardboard boxes lined with newspaper to dry.
Delilah Stoll   Sammie & Kathryn Schrock

E-Z OFF CLEANER

2 T. lye, heaping
1 tsp. cornstarch

1 c. cold water

Dissolve lye in 1/2 c. cold water. Mix cornstarch in 1/2 c. cold water and stir into lye mixture. Keep stirring until clear and thick. May be used on stainless steel, baked enamel (granite), iron and glass. Do not use on aluminum! Let soak for 30-60 minutes, then wash with vinegar water. Comes off like magic.
Yield: 1 c.

FLOOR POLISH

Put 1/4 cup of fabric softener in two gallons of warm mop water on varnished floors. This gives them a nice shine.

FLOOR CLEANER
Use washing soda from the grocery store. You may add Borax and boric acid (to deter insects except ants). Use white distilled vinegar in your rinse water for a natural shine and ant repellent. Do not add bleach to this. For the bathroom floor use plain bleach water - follow the label. Never use chlorine bleach if anybody in the home is ill or suffers from depression. Use grain alcohol (1 pint to 3 qt. Water) for germ killing action instead of chlorine.

FURNITURE DUSTER AND WINDOW CLEANER
Mix equal parts white distilled vinegar and water. Put it in a spray bottle.

FURNITURE POLISH
A few drops of olive oil on a dampened cloth. Use filtered water to dampen.

HOMEMADE SOAP
4 lbs. lard
1 can lye
1/2 c. ammonia

1/2 c. Borax
2 1/2 qt. water

Cold lard should be creamy (very important), then sprinkle lye over it. Add cold water, ammonia and Borax. Stir for 15 minutes or until smooth and thick. Pour in pans or boxes and cut as it hardens enough. This is not a very hard soap, but extra white.
Yield:
Virgil & Esther Yoder

INSECTS
To get rid of cabbage and cauliflower worms, steep garlic and catnip together in hot water. Apply two days in a row, then every 10 days.

Insects - How to expel them from trees:
Hang 2 bars homemade soap in the fork of fruit trees to ward off insects, etc. Or make a mixture of 1 pt. Vinegar, 1 pt. Sugar, 1 pt. Water. Divide this mixture into cut off jug bottoms or tops. Punch holes into jug pieces to hang in tree. Fasten strings. NOTE: Recycled (or used) pickle juice works super to attract insects and drown them in the vinegar.
Delilah Stoll

104

INSECT KILLER
Boric acid powder (not Borax). Throw liberal amounts behind stove, refrigerator, under carpets and in carpets. Since boric acid is white, you must be careful not to mistake it for sugar, accidentally. Keep it far away from food and out of children's reach. Buy it at a farm supply or garden store. It will not kill ants.

LAUNDRY CLEANER
Borax (1/2 c. per load). It is the main ingredient of nonchlorine bleach and has excellent cleaning power without fading colors. Your regular laundry soap may contain PCBs, aluminum, cobalt and other chemicals. These get rubbed into your skin constantly as you wear your clothing. For bleaching (only do this occasionally) use original chlorine bleach (not "new improved" or "with special brighteners," and so forth). Don't use chlorine if there is an ill person in the house. For getting out stubborn dirt at collars, scrub with homemade bar soap first; for stains, try grain alcohol, vinegar, baking soda.

MOTH BALLS
I found this recipe in an old recipe book. Mix the following and scatter in trunks and bags containing furs and woolens: 1/2 lb. each rosemary and mint, 1/4 lb. each tansy and thyme, 2 T. powdered cloves.

PLANT FOOD
1 tsp. baking powder   1/2 tsp. household ammonia
1 tsp. Epsom salts   1 gal. lukewarm water
1 tsp. salt petre
Stir together in the order given. Give to the plants in place of regular water every 4-6 weeks. Use especially on vines and ivys. Yield: 1 gal.
Glen & Sue Ellen Borkholder Sammie & Kathryn Schrock

RASPBERRY PLANT FOOD
1 gal. wood ashes   4 gal. lime
1 gal. Epsom salt   1 gal. sulfur
Mix all ingredients together. Put a handful to each berry stalk once a month in February, March, and April. Then once again when they have small berries, and again in the Fall. Can also mulch with leaves in fall.
Allen & Ruth Bontrager

SEEDS

Get your seeds off to a disease-free start by sprinkling Jello powder on them with a salt shaker (lightly - like you sprinkle salt on soup). Also, feed your young plants with Jello as they grow. The gelatin helps the plant hold water and the sugar feeds the organisms in the soil. Any flavor will do, but lemon is top choice because the citrus odor may repel some bugs.
Glen & Sue Ellen Borkholder

SHAMPOO

Borax liquid is ready to use as shampoo, too. It does not lather but goes right to work removing sweat and soil without stripping your color or natural oils. It inhibits scalp bacteria and stops flaking and itching. Hair gets squeaky clean so quickly (just a few squirts does it) that you might think nothing has happened! You will soon be accustomed to non-lathery soap. Rinse very thoroughly because you should leave your scalp slightly acidic. Take a pint container to the shower with you. Put 1/4 tsp. citric (not ascorbic) acid crystals in it. For long hair use a quart of rinse. Only citric acid is strong enough to get the Borax out, lemon juice and vinegar are not. After shampooing, fill the container with water and rinse. Rinse your whole body, too, since citric acid is also anti-bacterial. All hair shampoo penetrates the eyelids and gets into the eyes although you do not feel it. It is important to use this natural rinse to neutralize the shampoo in your eyes. (Some people have stated that citric acid makes their hair curlier or reddens it. If this is undesirable, use only half as much citric acid.) Citric acid also conditions and gives body and sheen to hair.

STOVE AND OVEN CLEANER

2 T. lye, heaping   1 T. cornstarch or flour
1 c. cold water

Dissolve lye in half of the water. In another container, mix cornstarch or flour in the other half of water. Pour starch solution slowly into the lye solution, stirring constantly. This cleaner may be used immediately or stored in a glass jar until required. Place newspaper on the floor under the stove. Spread the cleaner on stove surfaces using an old brush or sponge. Wash off with water and weak vinegar solution. The cleaner may be used on iron, steel and porcelain enamel. Do not use on painted surfaces or aluminum. Do not allow it to remain on skin or clothing. Rubber gloves are helpful. Do not breathe lye fumes.
Yield: 1 c.
Neal & Emma Yoder

TOMATO CURE

To ward off blight diseases that often afflict tomatoes, mix 1/4 cup of nonfat powdered milk with 1/4 cup of Epsom salts and a shovelful of compost. Sprinkle on baby plants when you set them out. Epsom salts + powdered milk + compost = happy tomatoes.
Glen & Sue Ellen Borkholder

TOMATO RIPENING

To hasten the ripening of garden tomatoes, put them in a brown paper bag. Close the bag and leave at room temperature for a few days.

A pickle is a cucumber soured by a jarring experience!

Plant onions with potatoes. They will "water their eyes."

When canning sweet corn; pack corn in jar, add 1 tsp. salt, 1 tsp. lemon juice to each qt., add water. Lemon seems to bring out the sweet flavor and it keeps better.

Have you ever tried a sugar snap pea canned? Try it! You might like it. Try Sugar Daddy or Sugar Ann, they're the best. Just remove the stem end, can pod and all.

When cutting onions, do not cut the roots off. This helps to prevent watery eyes.

To remove the core from a head of lettuce, hit the core end once against the counter, sharply. The core will loosen and pull out easily.

AIRPLANES
These are great treats at a party. Take one piece of gum for wings, two Lifesavers for wheels, and a Tootsie Roll or pack of Smarties for the body. Take a rubber band and put through both Lifesavers. Take both end loops and put the gum through for the wings. Slide your Tootsie Roll or pack of Smarties through for the body (between the Lifesaver wheels and under the wings).
Jacob Shetler

BREAKFAST BUFFET
An old Englishman I met in Africa was reminiscing about his exploration in earlier days, and the shock of one culture meeting another the first time. "Can you imagine," he said, "People so primitive that they love to eat the embryo of certain birds, and slices from the belly of certain animals? They grind up grass seed, make it into a paste, burn it over a fire, then smear it with a greasy mess they extract from the mammary fluid of animals?" While I shuddered at such barbarianism, he went on, "What I've been describing of course, is a breakfast of bacon and eggs and buttered toast."
Wayne & Kathryn Miller

COOKING A HUSBAND
A good many husbands are entirely spoiled by mismanagement in cooking and so are not tender and good. Some women keep them too constantly in hot water, others freeze them, others put them in a stew, and still others keep them constantly in a pickle. It cannot be supposed that any husband will be good and tender if managed in this way, but they are truly delicious if properly treated. Don't keep them in a kettle by force, as he will stay there himself if proper care is taken; if he should sputter and fizz, don't be anxious. Some husbands do this. Add a little sugar, the variety that confectioners call kisses. But on no account add vinegar and pepper! A little spice improves him, but it must be used with judgment. Do not try him with something sharp to see if he is becoming tender. Stir him gently, lest he lie too long in the kettle and become flat and tasteless. If you follow these directions, you will find him very digestible, agreeing nicely with you. And he will keep as you want to have him.
Jacob Shetler

Keep your words soft and sweet.
You never know when you'll have to eat them.

FUT NUDGE
2 buttlespoons of tabler
2 cups. shanulated gruger
3 cuppers quart of crin theam
2 chaws of squairkolet

2 sabel tunes of sorn keerup
1 nup of kelled shuts
1 vittle lanilla

Shook the kugar, the chilk, the mawkolet and the sorn keerup until the mawkolet chelts. Still without burring to 325 deheeze of gret, then dairfully crop a little of the mott hixture into a wawt of cold cupper. If a little bawft sawl forms in the cottum of the bupp . . . the didge is fun. Remove the hann from the peat, bad the utter, let canned until stool and fladd the aivoring. Speat with a boon until gick and thooey. Nopp in the druts, empty into a battered punn, and swark in mairs. You may marsh ad-mallows if you have a particularly tweet sooth. This serves a gruzzen doanups or two bean aged toys. -Colonel Stoopnagle

HAPPY TRASH
Take a large bowl or roaster and mix in all the *leftovers* (trash) from previous meals the cook is *happy* to get rid of and heat in the oven. Bingo! You have happy trash!
DeVon Miller

HUMMINGBIRD NECTAR
Mix one part sugar to three parts water. Add red or yellow food coloring.

MAGIC CHEMICAL GARDEN
Coal (a few pieces)
Water (in bowl)
6 tablespoons salt
3 tablespoons ammonia
6 tablespoons liquid bluing
6 tablespoons water
food coloring, optional
Put coal and a little water in a bowl. Mix salt, water, bluing and ammonia. Add food color by drops. Add slowly to the coal and water. Have fun watching it grow!
Delilah Stoll

By the time a man gets old enough to watch his step, he is too old to go anywhere.

MOM'S BEST PEANUT BUTTER COOKIES

1/2 c. granulated sugar	1 egg
1/2 c. brown sugar	Time
1 c. crunchy peanut butter	Love
1/2 c. chopped nuts	

Put a child on the counter so she can help you bake. Get out the egg and a bowl. Wipe up the egg that rolled off the counter. Get out another egg. Crack egg into the bowl. Answer the phone. Pour sugar into the bowl. Put the clothes in the dryer. Stir the sugar and egg together. Answer the door. Put the peanut butter in the bowl. Help the older child with homework. Stop the child who is helping, from sticking fingers in the bowl. Wipe peanut butter off the homework paper. Wipe tears. Put the nuts in the bowl. Mix well. Shape cookies into 1" balls. Roll in granulated sugar (the cookies, not you). Bake at 350º for 10 minutes. Serve cookies with milk, smiles and lots of love. Take a nap!
Jacob & Loretta Shetler

SCRIPTURE CAKE I

4 1/2 c. I Kings 4:22	2 c. Solomon 2:13
2 c. Jeremiah 6:20	2 c. Numbers 17:8
Pinch of Leviticus 2:13	2 T. I Samuel 14:25
6 Isaiah 10:14, beaten	Spices:
1/2 c. Judges 4;19	2 tsp. cloves
2 tsp. I Corinthians 5:6	4 tsp. cinnamon
8 1/2 tsp. II Chronicles 9:9	1/2 tsp. nutmeg
1 1/2 tsp. Psalms 55:21	2 tsp. allspice
2 c. II Samuel 16;1	

Follow instructions in Proverbs 23:14. Pour batter in greased bread pans and bake for 50 minutes at 325º. Cool and slice after a few John 11:9.
Ruby Miller

SCRIPTURE CAKE II

1 c. Judges 5:25	2 T. I Samuel 14:25
2 c. Jeremiah 6:20	1/2 c. Judges 4:19
6 Isaiah 10:14, beaten	2 c. Samuel 30:12
4 1/2 c. I Kings 4:22	2 c. Nahum 3:12
2 tsp. Amos 4:25	1 c. Numbers 17:8
1 pinch Leviticus 2:13	

Cream butter and sugar. Add well-beaten egg yolks. Sift flour, baking powder, and salt together. Add alternately with mixture of honey and milk. Beat well. Add: Raisins, figs and almonds which have been coated with flour. Fold in stiffly beaten egg whites. Pour in greased tube pan. Bake at 350º for 1 1/4 hours.
Ruby Miller

PRESERVING CHILDREN

Take one large grassy field and one-half dozen children, all sizes. Add one dog and one long narrow strip of brook. Mix children with other ingredients and empty them into the field, stirring continually. Sprinkle with field flowers. Pour the brook gently over pebbles. Cover all with a deep blue sky and bake in the hot sun. When children are well browned, they may be removed. They will be found ready to cool in a bathtub with lots of soap and water.
Herman & Carolina Miller

LOVELY LETTER

My sweet potato, Do you carrot all for me?
You are the apple of my eye With your radish hair and turnip nose.
My heart beets for you. My love for you is as strong as onions.
If we cantaloupe, lettuce marry, And we will be a happy pear!

PRESERVING A HUSBAND

Be careful in your selection. Do not choose too young, and take only such as have been reared in a good moral atmosphere. Some insist on keeping them in a pickle, while others keep them in hot water. This only makes them sour, hard and sometimes bitter. Even poor varieties may be made sweet, tender and good b y garnishing them with patience, well sweetened with smiles and flavored with kisses, to taste. Then wrap them in a mantle of charity. Keep them warm with a steady fire of domestic devotion and serve with peaches and cream. When thus prepared, they will keep for years.
Herman & Carolina Miller

LIFE'S RECIPE

One cup of good thoughts, 1 cup of kind deeds, 1 cup of consideration for others, 2 cups sacrifice for others, 3 cups of forgiveness and 2 cups of well beaten faults. Mix these thoroughly and add joy and sorrow and sympathy for others. Flavor with gifts of love. Fold in 4 cups of prayer and faith to lighten other ingredients and raise the texture to a great height of Christian living. After pouring all this into your daily life, bake well with the heart of human kindness. Serve with a smile.
Jacob & Loretta Shetler

Kind words can be short and easy to speak, but their echoes are truly endless.

HEAVEN'S GROCERY STORE

I was walking down life's highway a long time ago. One day I saw a sign that read, HEAVEN'S GROCERY STORE. As I got a little closer, the door came open wide, and when I came to myself, I was standing inside. I saw a host of ANGELS. They were standing everywhere. One handed me a basket and said, My child, shop with care. Everything a Christian needs was in that grocery store. And all you couldn't carry, you could come back the next day for more. First, I got some PATIENCE. LOVE was in the same row. Further down was UNDERSTANDING: you need that everywhere you go. I got a box or two of WISDOM, a bag or two of FAITH. I just couldn't miss the HOLY GHOST; for it was all over the place. I stopped to get some STRENGTH and COURAGE to help me run this race. By then my basket was getting full, but I remembered I needed some GRACE. I didn't forget SALVATION, for SALVATION was free, so I tried to get enough of that to save both you and me. Then I started up to the counter to pay my grocery bill, for I thought I had everything to do the Master's will. As I went up the aisle, I saw PRAYER, and I just had to put that in, for I knew when I stepped outside, I would run into sin. PEACE and JOY were plentiful; they were the last on the shelf. SONG and PRAISE were hanging near, so I just helped myself. Then I said to the angel, How much do I owe? He smiled and said, Just take them everywhere you go. Again, I smiled and said, How much do I really owe? He smiled again and said, MY CHILD, JESUS PAID YOUR BILL A LONG, LONG TIME AGO. ALL THINGS WHATSOEVER YOU SHALL ASK IN PRAYER, BELIEVING, YOU SHALL RECEIVE. (Matthew 21:22)

ROSE OF LIFE

The rose of colorful hues Like to sparkle in the dew,
The colorful petals so fair Send their fragrance in the air;
And then on the short summer's end, The lovely hues that so blend
Will silently float to the ground In starchy petals of brown;
But they play an important part In their little crimson heart...
Our short life is just like the rose While we're toiling here below,
The bud is where we start our goal- When our childhood starts to mold,
And when petals are downward sent- Our short life is then well spent,
Thus we all hope to join the throng In heaven and sing God's songs.
Rebecca Miller (Wayne) Grade 8 - 1996

Hail to the girl who has learned the art
Of cooking her way to her husband's heart.
She gives him roasts and pies for dinner;
He could be happier, but he could be thinner!

SHUT-IN CHEER UP LETTER
On a white poster, tape each candy bar in the appropriate spot in this letter.

Dear Friend,
I'd love to give you <u>100 Grand</u> as a get well wish, but the money slipped through my <u>Butterfinger</u>. We could hop on a <u>Dove</u>, fly to the <u>Milky Way</u> and to <u>Mars</u>. Or go down <u>5th Avenue</u>, and look for <u>Baby Ruth</u>, but it's not <u>Pay Day</u>, so neither seems appropriate. I wish you <u>Mounds</u> of <u>Almond Joy</u> as you <u>Zero</u> in on a full recovery. <u>P.S.</u> <u>Mr. Goodbar</u> promised not to <u>Snicker</u>, but you better hide this from your <u>Pa</u>. Give him this old <u>Clark</u> bar if he promises not to play anymore of his <u>Twix.</u> From: Miss <u>Watchamacallit.</u>

EASTER JELLY BEANS
Red is for the blood He gave,
Green is for the grass He made,
Yellow is for His sun so bright,
Orange is for the edge of night,
Black is for the sins we made,
White is for the grace He gave,
Purple is for His sorrow,
Pink is for our new tomorrow,
A bag of jelly beans, colorful and sweet,
Is a prayer, is a promise, is a Special Treat!

Mrs.: "Do you love me still?"
Mr.: "Yes, better than any other way."

JAMS, JELLIES & SPREADS

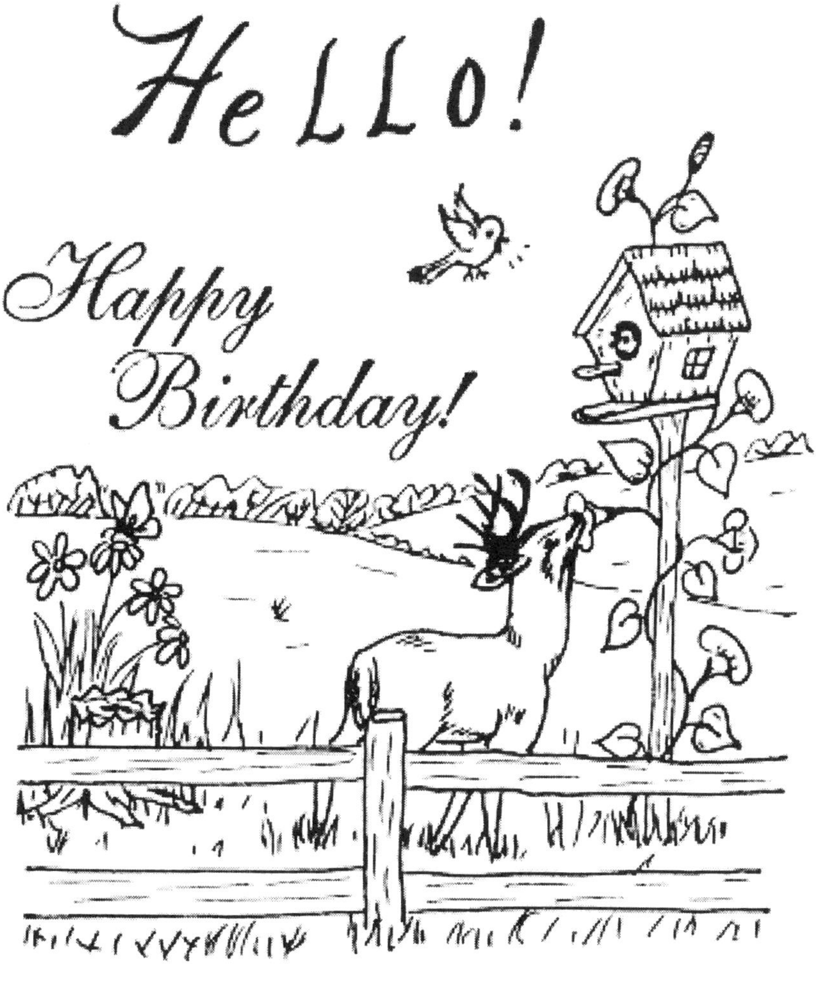

APPLE BUTTER

9 qt. applesauce	Salt
2 c. brown sugar	1 1/2 tsp. allspice
2 c. white sugar	1 tsp. cinnamon
1/2 c. vinegar	

Mix allspice and cinnamon with small amount of sauce and add last. This is for a stainless steel cooker full of applesauce. I have my Aunt Lydia's (Emery) recipe box and this was in it and signed Wm. P. Emma. Grandma could always make good apple butter. Grandpa would pile it on his bread by dipping his knife into the apple butter and then wiping the knife off on his bread. He always did this before every bite of bread.
Sammie & Kathryn Schrock

During the Great Depression, our grandparents, William and Emma lived near Wasepi where our uncle Roman yet lives. Their lane crossed a railroad tracks. The depressed economy caused many men to leave their families in search of work. These "hobos" often traveled from one place to another by hitching a ride in an empty train car. Many of them stopped by our grandparents place asking for something to eat. Grandma always fixed them a piece of bread, spread with her famous apple butter. Above is the recipe. -DM

APPLE BUTTER II

4 gal. cut up apples	1 T. cinnamon
1 gal. Karo	1 tsp. nutmeg
5-6 lbs. sugar	1 tsp. allspice

Put this in a cooker in the evening and put lid on. Next morning, put it on stove. After you hear it boiling, boil it for 3 hours without removing lid. Other spices can be added as you wish.
Yield: Approx. 15 qt.
Wayne & Kathryn Miller

APPLE BUTTER III

8 qt. applesauce	2 tsp. cinnamon
12 c. sugar	1 tsp. cloves

Put applesauce in a roaster in the oven. When it has cooked down some, add sugar and spices. Cook 5-6 more hours or until it is thickened like you want it.
Herman & Carolina Miller

One's love for God is equal to the love one has for the man he loves least.

HOT PEPPER BUTTER

40 semi-hot peppers
1 c. onion
1 pt. vinegar
2 1/2 lbs. brown sugar

1 qt. mustard
1 c. flour
3 T. salt, scant

Remove seeds from peppers and put through a grinder. Grind onions. Add all ingredients in a large kettle. Simmer 15 minutes, stirring constantly. Make a sauce with the flour and a little water, then stir into the first mixture and simmer 5 minutes longer. This is good as is, but we like it with 1 qt. of salad dressing added.
Yield:
Joni & Emma Sue Miller

GRANOLA PEANUT BUTTER

6 c. oatmeal
3 c. bran
1 1/2 c. wheat germ
1 1/2 c. coconut
1 1/2 c. nuts, if desired

1 1/2 - 2 c. mixed peanut butter (church peanut butter)
1/2 c. vegetable oil
1 tsp. vanilla

Mix dry ingredients. Add peanut butter, oil, vanilla and mix thoroughly and toast in 350° until lightly browned. Keep stirred.
NOTE: Wheat germ is best fresh. If caked or bitter, it is not fresh. Use old wheat germ in baked goods. It makes them softer and gives a better flavor.
Yield: 13 cups
Delilah Stoll

MAPLE CREAM SPREAD

7 c. brown sugar
1 c. water

7 c. thick corn syrup
10 egg whites

Bring the first three ingredients to a rolling boil. Beat the egg whites until stiff. Add this to the slightly cooled syrup slowly, beating constantly until thoroughly mixed and until cool. Add maple flavoring to suit taste. Peanut butter can be added to make church spread.
Jacob & Loretta Shetler

PEANUT BUTTER SPREAD FOR CHURCH

2 lbs. crunchy or smooth peanut butter
2 qt. light Karo

2 qt. marshmallow topping
1 T. vanilla

Mix until smooth. Add water if too thick or omit vanilla and use maple syrup instead of water.
Delilah Stoll

PEANUT BUTTER

Use fresh unsalted roasted peanuts - they will be white on the first day they arrive at the health food store from the distributor. (Ask when they will arrive.) Or shell fresh roasted peanuts yourself, throwing away all shriveled or darkened nuts. Grind, adding salt and vitamin C (1/4 tsp. per pint) as you go. For spreadability, especially for children, grind an equal volume of cold butter along with the peanuts. This improves spreadability and digestibility of the hard nut particles. This will probably be the most heavenly peanut butter your mouth has ever experienced.

RED BEET JELLY

6 c. beet juice
1/2 c. lemon juice
2 pkg. Sure Jell

8 c. sugar
6 oz. pkg. raspberry Jello

Cook red beets and prick them to make juice. Bring beet juice, lemon juice and Sure Jell to a hard boil. Add sugar and Jello. Stir well. Boil six minutes. Put in jars to seal.
Yield: 5-6 pt.
Allen & Ruth Bontrager

RHUBARB JAM

5 c. rhubarb
5 c. sugar
1/3 c. water

1 c. crushed pineapple
1 box (6 oz.) Jello (any flavor)

Cut rhubarb very fine and scald with boiling water. Drain. Add sugar and water. Boil 12 minutes. Add pineapple, boil three minutes longer. Take off the heat. Add Jello and stir well. Put in jars and seal.

ROSY RHUBARB PRESERVES

5 c. rhubarb, cut fine
1 c. crushed pineapple
4 c. sugar

1 T. gelatin, dissolved in cold water
Jello (strawberry)

Cook the rhubarb, pineapple and sugar, stirring often. Cook over medium heat until mixture becomes clear and thick; about 10-20 minutes. Remove and stir in gelatin and Jello.
Yield: 3 1/2 pt.
Sammie & Kathryn Schrock

Love has power to give in a moment what toil can scarcely reach in an age.

There is no better exercise for the heart than reaching out and lifting people up.

SANDWICH SPREAD

6 green peppers
9 red peppers
6 green tomatoes
4 mild onions
3 c. vinegar

3 T. salt
2 c. brown sugar
3 T. mustard
1 qt. salad dressing

Grind the peppers, tomatoes and onions together. Cover with boiling water and let stand ten minutes. Drain well. Add the vinegar, salt, and brown sugar. Cook for eight more minutes. To thicken add the mustard and salad dressing. Can also add 6 T. flour with water. Allow to stand a few minutes. Seal in jelly jars or qt. jars while hot. Great for lunches.
Yield:
Alva & Katie Ann Bontrager

SPREADING CHEESE

1 gal. thick milk
1/2 tsp. baking soda
1/2 c. butter
2 eggs

1 T. sugar
1 1/2 c. cream or milk
Salt

Heat milk to 120º to scald, stirring often. Let stand at room temperature for 30 minutes. Drain through a cloth overnight. Crumb the curds and add baking soda and butter. Let stand for two hours. Place in a double boiler. Add eggs, sugar, cream or milk, and salt. Stir often. Melt until fairly smooth. Can also add a jar of Cheez Whiz or cheddar cheese powder.
Yield: Approx. 1 1/2 qt.
Sammie & Kathryn Schrock

ZUCCHINI PRESERVES

6c ups zucchini, peeled and ground
1/4 c. lemon juice
1 c. crushed pineapple, undrained
4 c. white sugar
1 pkg. (6 oz.) or 3/4 c. Jello

Peel and grind the zucchini. Bring slowly to a boil. Do not add water. Boil 12-15 minutes. Add lemon juice, pineapple and sugar. Boil 15 minutes. Take off stove and add Jello - any flavor. Apricot is real good; or use half orange and half lemon. Put in jars and seal.
Yield: 2 qt.
Allen & Ruth Bontrager

To be content with little is difficult, to be content with much is impossible.

Congratulations on your Wedding Day

May you always find happiness together!

ASPARAGUS CHEESE DISH

8 pieces bread, buttered
8 oz. cheddar cheese, shredded
3 c. cooked asparagus

2 c. ham, cubed
6 eggs
3 c. milk
1/2 tsp. salt

Place buttered bread face down in a 9 X 13 pan. Sprinkle with shredded cheese, spread asparagus and ham on top. Beat eggs, milk and salt together. Pour over layers in pan. Bake at 325° for 50 minutes. Sprinkle with remaining cheese and return to oven until done.
Yield: 9 x 13 pan
David & Mary Kauffman

BAKED SQUASH

1 med. butternut squash
3-4 apples
1/2 c. brown sugar
1/4 c. margarine, melted

1 T. flour
1/2 tsp. salt
1/2 tsp. mace

Cut up the squash and the apples. Mix the rest of the ingredients and pour over the top. Bake 50-60 minutes at 350°.
Yield: Approx. 8 servings
Monroe & Elsie Miller

BEEF NACHO CASSEROLE

1 lb. ground beef
1 sm. onion
1 jar (12 oz.) chunky salsa
1 sm. pkg. frozen corn or 1 can sweet corn
1 c. sour cream
1 can Mexican chili beans
2 c. tortilla chips, crushed
2 c. cheddar cheese, shredded

Brown meat with chopped onion. Stir in corn, salsa, sour cream and chili beans. Layer half of the meat mixture, chips and cheese. Repeat layers, keeping cheese back until last 15 minutes of baking time. Bake at 350° for 30 minutes or until heated through.
Joni & Emma Sue Miller

CHICKEN CASSEROLE

2 c. Minute rice
Chicken pieces
Mix together:
1 pkg. onion soup mix

1 can mushroom soup
1 can celery soup
1 c. water

Pour this mixture over the rice and chicken and bake at 350° for 1 1/2 hours.
Herman & Carolina Miller

BROCCOLI RICE CASSEROLE

Raw or frozen broccoli
2 c. rice, cooked
2 lbs. fried hamburger with onion
1 can cream of mushroom soup
1 can cream of chicken soup
1 can cream of celery soup
1 c. Velveeta cheese
Salt and pepper to taste
Milk for desired thickness
Tater Tots

Melt cheese in milk and soups. Cook broccoli until about half done. Mix together and put in a roaster; spread tater tots on top. Bake at 350º for one hour or until tater tots are browned.
Joni & Emma Sue Miller

CABBAGE GOULASH

1 lg. head of cabbage
1 1/2 lbs. bulk sausage or sliced smoky links
2 sm. yellow summer squash
1 can hot chili beans
1 sm. onion
1 green pepper
1 jar salsa
1 1/2 c. cheddar cheese

Shred cabbage and put in a large kettle. Fry sausage with onion and green pepper until done. If smoky links are used, saute onion and pepper in butter. Cook diced squash until done. Add all ingredients to cabbage and simmer until cabbage is crisp tender.
Joni & Emma Sue Miller

CHEESEBURGER BAKE

1 lb. ground beef
3/4 c. chopped onion
1 can (10 3/4 oz.) condensed cheddar cheese soup
1 c. frozen mixed vegetables
1/4 c. milk
2 c. Bisquick
3/4 c. water
1 c. shredded cheddar cheese

Heat oven to 400º. Grease 9 X 13 baking pan. Brown the beef and onion, drain. Stir in soup, vegetables and milk. Stir Bisquick and water in baking pan; spread evenly. Spread beef mixture over batter. Bake 30 minutes. Sprinkle with cheese.
Paul & Rhonda Borkholder

Rub vinegar on hands and dry before hanging clothes out in cold weather to keep hands from getting so cold. Repeat as necessary.

CHICKEN RICE CASSEROLE

1 c. rice
1 c. water
Chicken, cut up

1 can mushroom soup
1 can cream of chicken soup
1 pkg. dry onion soup

Mix all together and pour into 9 X 13 pan. Bake, covered for 1 hour or until rice is soft. Top with cheese, if desired.
Mabel (DeVon) Miller

DRESSING

1 gal. toasted bread cubes
1 c. chopped celery
1 c. chopped onions
1 c. chopped carrots
1 c. cut chicken meat
5 beaten eggs

1 T. celery seed
2 T. parsley flakes
2 T. spiced salt (vega-salt)
Salt
Pepper
1 qt. milk

Heat 1 qt. chicken broth and add 1 stick butter. When melted, pour over toast, vegetables and seasonings. Beat eggs and milk together and also add. Mix all together and bake at 325° until set. Add more broth or milk if it seems too thick.
Raymond & Martha Bontrager

FARMER'S CORN CASSEROLE

1 egg
1/4 c. butter
3/4 c. sour cream
1 can whole corn, drained
1 can creamed corn

1/4 tsp. salt
1/2 c. milk
8 oz. corn muffin mix
1 c. cheddar cheese

In a bowl, beat the egg and add the butter and sour cream. Stir in the corn, salt and milk. Add the muffin mix. Pour in a greased baking dish and top with cheese. Bake, uncovered, at 350° for one hour.
Yield:
David & Mary Kauffman

FAST NOODLES

Put 4 lbs. all-purpose in a large bowl. Beat 1 qt. egg yolk lightly into 1 1/2 c. boiling water. Pour over flour, mix the best you can. Sprinkle flour over top. Let stand 20 min. Take out and finish working into cakes. Put through noodle maker or roll out and cut into strips and shapes. Children love to cut their own noodles. Especially if they get too dry to put through cutter. They can use cookie cutters to make shapes, etc.
Delilah Stoll

GOURMET POTATOES

12 medium potatoes
2 c. grated cheddar or Velveeta cheese
1/4 c. butter
2/3 c. chopped onions
1/2 c. sour cream
Salt and pepper
1 can cream of mushroom soup
3 c. crushed cracker crumbs, browned in 1/2 c. butter
Cook potatoes in their skins, cool. Peel and shoestring in a saucepan over low heat. Combine cheese and butter; stir occasionally until almost melted. Remove from heat and blend in sour cream, onion and seasoning. Fold in potatoes and turn into greased casserole dish. Top with browned cracker crumbs and bake 30 minutes, uncovered.
Yield:
Virgil & Esther Yoder

HAYSTACK SUPPER

Ritz crackers, crumbled
Lettuce, cut up
Hamburger, browned
Pizza sauce, heated
Rice, (plain) cooked
Jacob & Loretta Shetler

Cheese sauce, heated
Doritos, crumbled
Fix on your plate in the order given.

HOT DOG KRAUT CASSEROLE

5-6 med. potatoes with skins, cooked
1 lb. hot dogs, cut in small pieces
1/2 c. mayonnaise
1/2 c. mushroom soup
1 - 16 oz. can sour kraut
Mix together and put in the bottom of a casserole. Take the other half of the mushroom soup and mix with sliced potatoes. Mix and put on top of the first part, do not stir. Take 1/2 c. melted butter and add enough bread crumbs to soak up. Put on top and bake for one hour at 350º
Herman & Carolina Miller

I sometimes use cake batter, put in cupcake tins for quick cupcakes. Provides some variety in lunches.

NAVAJO TACOS

1 lb. hamburger, fried and seasoned
1 - 15 oz. can ranch-style or chili hot beans
Simmer together for 15 minutes
Crush 1 bag tortilla chips
Shred 1/2 head of lettuce
Grate 1/2 lb. mild cheddar cheese
Dice 2 med. tomatoes
Dice 1 c. onions
Prepare all foods. Make a cheese sauce. Then stack different items on your plate like a haystack with meat mixture last. Then cover everything with cheese sauce.
Raymond & Martha Bontrager

OVERNIGHT MACARONI CASSEROLE

2 c. cooked chicken
2 c. uncooked macaroni shells
2 cans cream of chicken soup
2 c. milk
1/2 T. salt
1/2 medium onion, chopped
1/4 T. pepper
3 T. butter
1 c. grated cheese

It's best to melt cheese with seasonings, milk and soup. Let cool. When cook, pour over remaining ingredients. Mix and put in a greased casserole. Let set overnight and bake 1 1/2 hours at 350°.
Yield: 6-8 servings
Amos & Elizabeth Miller

PAN GRAVY

1/2 c. Crisco (vegetable shortening) melted
1 c. flour
1 - 10 1/2 oz. can mushroom soup
2 1/2 to 3 (10 1/2 oz.) liquid seasoning salt for flavoring
Mix the Crisco in a saucepan, then add the flour and brown it to a color desired. Mix together in a bowl the mushroom soup and liquid and pour into saucepan. Stir and season.
Wayne & Kathryn Miller

PENSEY SUPPER

4 lg. potatoes
1 pt. peas
6 hot dogs, sliced
1 can mushroom soup
1 sm. onion, chopped
1 T. mustard
1/4 c. butter
Salt to taste
Pepper to taste

Cook potatoes; cut in small squares. Add the rest of the ingredients. Put in casserole and bake one hour.
Joni & Emma Sue Miller

PAPRIKA POTATOES

1/2 c. butter
1/4 c. flour
1/4 c. parmesan cheese
1 T. paprika

3/4 tsp. salt
1/8 tsp. pepper
Pinch garlic or onion salt
6 med. potatoes, cut in wedges

Melt butter in a 9 X 13 baking pan. Combine next 6 ingredients in a bag; set aside. Rinse potatoes under cold water, drain well. Place half of potatoes in bag, shake well to coat. Place in a single layer in pan. Repeat with remaining potatoes. Bake uncovered at 350º for 50-60 minutes or until tender, turning once at 30 minutes.
Paul & Rhonda Borkholder

PIZZA BUBBLES

1 qt. spaghetti sauce
1 qt. hamburger or sausage
1 roll crescent rolls
Peppers

Onions
Mushrooms
Pepperoni
Cheese

Put spaghetti sauce in a bowl and add hamburger or sausage, peppers, onions, mushrooms and pepperoni. Stir. Cut crescent rolls in smaller pieces and add. Stir all together and pour into a roaster. Bake at 400º for 20 minutes. Remove from oven and add your favorite cheese. Return to oven till cheese is melted. Delicious!
Joni & Emma Sue Miller

PIZZA DUMPLINGS

1 lb. ground hamburger
4 c. pizza sauce
1 green pepper
        Dumplings:
1 c. flour
1 1/2 tsp. baking powder
1/2 tsp. salt

1 onion, chopped
1/4 c. chopped celery

1/2 tsp. basil
1 T. butter
2/3 c. milk

In a skillet, saute onion, green pepper and celery. Add hamburger and brown thoroughly. Add pizza sauce and simmer for 5-10 minutes. Meanwhile, for dumplings, combine flour, baking powder, and salt in a bowl. Cut in butter and add milk and basil. Drop by tablespoons into bubbling sauce mixture. Cover tightly and simmer for 12-15 minutes. Remove. Top with grated cheddar.
Yield: 6 servings
Virgil & Esther Yoder

Egg shells can be easily removed from hard-boiled eggs if they are quickly rinsed in cold water first.

PIZZA CRUST WITH SAUCE SUPREME

Crust:
1 pkg. active dry yeast
1 3/4 c. warm water (110º)
3 T. salad oil
1 T. honey
1 tsp. salt
4 c. unsifted all-purpose flour

Sauce:
1 med. onion, chopped
1 clove garlic, minced or pressed
1 T. salad oil
1 T. oregano
2 T. parsley
Salt and pepper, to taste
2 - 8 oz. cans tomato sauce

Dissolve yeast in warm water in large bowl; beat in the oil, salt, and honey. Add flour and beat in enough additional flour (about 1 cup) to form a stiff dough. Turn onto a well-floured board and knead it until smooth, about 3 minutes. Put dough into a greased bowl; cover it and let rise in a warm place until it doubles in size. Punch down the dough and divide it into thirds for thin crust or halves for thicker crust. Roll, pat, and stretch dough to fit pizza pan, remembering to form an edge. Bake on the lowest rack in 500(oven for about 5 minutes for thin crust or about 7 minutes for thick crust. Spread the baked crust with sauce and condiments and bake again on lowest rack of 500(oven for 5-8 minutes. Sauce: Saute the onion and garlic in oil until onion is limp and golden; add tomato sauce and seasonings. Simmer for 15 minutes, stirring often. Suggestion: Zip the pizza under the broiler for about 1 minute to give the cheese a golden crust.

PIZZA DOUGH

1 pkg. yeast
1 tsp. sugar
1 tsp. salt
2 pkg. yeast

1 1/2 c. warm water
3 - 3 1/2 c. flour
2 T. Mazola oil

Stir together yeast, salt and sugar. Dissolve in warm. Add Mazola oil and flour, let rise for 20 min. Press into 12 X 18 cookie sheet or 2 round pizza pans.
Mabel (DeVon) Miller

POTATO SALAD DRESSING

Bring to a boil:
1/2 c. vinegar
1 T. butter
Add:
2 eggs, beaten
Joni & Emma Sue Miller

3/4 c. sugar
1 T. mustard
1/2 tsp. salt
2 c. salad dressing

PIZZA PIE

3 eggs
3/4 c. Bisquick
1/2 tsp. salt
1 1/2 c. milk

3 c. meat
1 can mushrooms
Shredded cheese
Pizza sauce

Put a layer of meat in the bottom of a greased pan. Any combination can be used - browned hamburger, sausage, ham, etc. Layer mushrooms on top of meat. Beat together first four ingredients and pour over the meat carefully. Bake at 350º until firm - about 45 minutes. Spread pizza sauce on top, then sprinkle on cheese. Put back in oven until cheese is melted.
Yield: 2 pies
David & Mary Kauffman

SOUR CREAM ENCHILADAS

1 lb. ground beef (or more)
1 sm. onion
1/2 tsp. salt
2 T. butter
2 tsp. chicken base
4 T. flour

2 c. water
2 c. sour cream
1 can green chilies
10-12 tortillas
1/2 c. cheddar cheese, shredded
1 c. mozzarella cheese, shredded

Brown beef with onion and salt. Meanwhile boil water, flour, soup base and butter until slightly thickened. Remove from heat and stir in sour cream and chills. Mix some sour cream mixture with the beef. Put on a tortilla and roll up. Put on a cookie sheet. Put a layer of sour cream mixture over all the tortillas, and bake at 350º until bubbly. Coat with another layer of mixture, top with cheese and put back in the oven until cheese is melted.
Yield: 10-12 servings
Glen & Sue Ellen Borkholder

SPINACH NOODLE BAKE

1 lb. Innmaid noodles
6-8 c. shredded spinach
1 can mushroom soup
1 can cream of chicken soup
1 can salmon
2 sm. cans mushrooms
1 can ripe olives, sliced
2 eggs, beaten
2 c. baby Swiss or mozzarella cheese
Lemon pepper, to taste
Salt, to taste
Cook noodles until done. Cook spinach until wilted. Debone and flake salmon. Combine all ingredients and bake one hour at 350º.
Joni & Emma Sue Miller

SWEET POTATO CASSEROLE

3 c. cooked and mashed sweet potatoes
1/2 c. butter
1/2 c. sugar
2 eggs, beaten
1 tsp. vanilla

Topping:
1/2 c. flour
2/3 c. brown sugar
1/3 c. butter, softened
1 c. pecans, chopped

Mix first 5 ingredients together and put in buttered baking dish. Combine the remaining ingredients and sprinkle on top. Sprinkle 1/2 c. pecans on top of entire mixture. Bake covered at 350º for 45 minutes or until golden brown. This is a wonderful addition to your Thanksgiving dinner.
Yield: 1 - 9 X 13 pan
Linda (Willis) Bontrager   Oba & Laura Borkholder
Neal & Emma Yoder   Glen & Sue Ellen Borkholder

SWEET POTATO APPLE CASSEROLE

1 1/4 lbs. sweet potatoes
1/2 c. water
1 lb. apples
1 c. apple juice

2 T. cornstarch
3 T. water
1/2 c. honey
1/3 c. wheat germ

In a pot with a tight fitting lid, steam sweet potatoes in 1/2 c. water until tender, 15 to 20 minutes. Peel and slice them lengthwise in 1/2" thick slices. Layer them in a casserole. Peel and core apples, slicing them 1/2" thick. Lay apple slices on top of sweet potatoes. Heat apple juice to the boiling point. Combine cornstarch and water and add juice, cooking until sauce is clear and thickened. Add honey. Spoon over apples, then top with wheat germ. Bake in a 350º oven until apples are tender, 30-60 minutes.
Yield: 6 servings

TACO CASSEROLE

1 lb. ground beef
2/3 c. salad dressing
1 c. shredded cheese
2 c. Bisquick

3-4 med. tomatoes, chopped
1 c. sour cream
2 T. chopped onion
1 c. chopped green pepper

Cook and stir beef until brown. Drain it and mix sour cream, salad dressing, cheese and onions. Mix Bisquick and water until soft dough forms. Pat into a 9 X 13 pan pressing 1/2" up the sides. Layer beef, tomatoes and peppers in pan. Spoon sour cream mixture over top. Bake until edges of dough are light brown, 25-30 minutes. Pizza dough can be used instead of Bisquick and water.
Menno & Malinda Miller

TURKEY DRESSING CASSEROLE

3/4 c. melted butter
2 tsp. salt
1/2 - 1 tsp. Accent
1/4 tsp. pepper
1 tsp. sage or 1/2 tsp. each thyme, rosemary and marjoram
2 qt. soft bread cubes
3/4 c. milk
1/3 c. chopped onion
1/3 c. chopped celery with leaves
Leftover turkey, cooked
For Gravy:
Mix together first 5 ingredients. Lightly toss seasoned butter with a mixture of remaining ingredients, except turkey and gravy. Layer dressing, turkey, then gravy in casserole. Bake at 350º for about 45 minutes.

VEGETABLE PIZZA

Pizza crust dough
1 pkg. Hidden Valley Ranch mix
2 c. mayonnaise or sour cream
1/4 c. milk
Variety of chopped raw vegetables
Colby cheese, grated
Use your own pizza crust recipe, using less flour. Bisquick mix is fine. Mix the dressing, mayonnaise and milk. Pour over the baked pizza crust. Use any vegetables you have handy: carrots, celery, pickles, broccoli, tomatoes, peppers, cauliflower; whatever is in season. Sprinkle it over the pizza crust. Top with plenty of grated Colby cheese and ham, hard boiled eggs, mushrooms. . . go wild! In the winter when raw vegetables are scarce, I like to put dill pickles on top with Velveeta cheese and put in the oven long enough to melt the cheese.
Jacob & Loretta Shetler

ZUCCHINI SAUSAGE CASSEROLE

1 lb. browned sausage
4 c. zucchini, diced
1/2 c. mushroom soup
2 eggs, beaten
14 crackers, crushed
1/2 onion, diced
1 tsp. salt
Sprinkle of pepper
1 c. shredded cheddar cheese
Mix together all ingredients except the cheese. Pour into a greased casserole dish and top with cheese. Bake uncovered for one hour at 325º.
Yield:
David & Mary Kauffman

Thinking of You

HOMEMADE MAPLE SYRUP

2 c. brown sugar
2 c. white sugar
1 c. white Karo
1/2 tsp. maple flavoring
1 c. water
Boil together for 5 minutes at low heat.
Raymond & Martha Bontrager

PANCAKE SYRUP

Bring 1 cup water to a boil and add 2 cups sugar; stir until dissolved.
Add:
1 T. molasses
1 tsp. maple flavoring
1/2 tsp. butter flavoring
Simmer to desired consistency.
Yield: 1 3/4 cups

RUBY'S PANCAKE SYRUP

1 c. brown sugar
1/2 Perma flow
1/2 c. water
Mix ingredients together and stir into:
5 c. boiling water
Vanilla
Pinch of salt
This syrup is not nearly as sweet but still delicious. Diabetic exchange – instead of adding sugar, add 4 drops of stevia liquid.
Yield: 1 1/2 qt.
Ruby Miller

BARBEQUED MEATBALLS

2 lbs. ground beef
1 lb. ground pork (or gr. beef)
2 c. milk (or evaporated milk)
2 c. quick oatmeal
1 c. cracker crumbs
1/2 tsp. pepper
      Sauce:
2 c. ketchup
1 1/2 c. brown sugar
1 T. Liquid Smoke

2 tsp. chili powder
1/2 tsp. garlic powder
2-3 tsp. salt
2 eggs
1/2 c. chopped onions

1/2 tsp. garlic powder
1/2 c. chopped onions

Mix the meat, milk, oatmeal, eggs, onions and seasonings together. Form into walnut size balls. Mix sauce together and pour over meatballs. Bake at 350º for one hour.
Yield: Approx. 80 walnut-sized meatballs
Amos & Elizabeth Miller   Virgil & Esther Yoder   Linda   (Willis) Bontrager

BEEF JERKY

1/2 c. salt
1/2 c. brown sugar
1/4 c. soy sauce
1 heaping T. black pepper

Pinch of red pepper
1/2 c. Liquid Smoke or hickory
seasoning
1/2 gal. water

If more than 10-12 lbs. of meat is used, make a double portion. Put all ingredients with thin strips of meat in a tub or five gallon bucket and mix. Soak for 18-24 hours. Stir occasionally. Drain. Usually you can use the liquid twice. To dry the meat, put a wire rack about 4" above a wood stove or other comparable situation. Very good!
Nathan O. Borkholder

BOLOGNA

50 lbs. ground beef
2 1/2 T. Liquid Smoke
1 tsp. coriander
1/2 tsp. mace
1 1/2 tsp. red pepper

1 1/8 lb. Tenderquick
3 qt. water
1 1/2 c. brown sugar
1 tsp. paprika
1 T. black pepper

2 tsp. salt petre, optional (the bologna is drier without this)
Mix all ingredients with water before adding to meat. Do not use different meat for bologna; just grind hamburger twice. Process at ten lb. pressure for one hour.
Yield: 24-25 qt.
Oba & Laura Borkholder

CHICKEN BOLOGNA

50 lbs. raw meat
1 lb. tenderquick
1 oz. coriander powder
1 T. black pepper
1 tsp. salt petre

1 T. garlic salt or powder
2 lbs. water
1/2 lb. salt
5 T. liquid smoke
1 tsp. mace

Grind the meat, (after cutting the meat off the bones) tenderquick, salt and salt petre together twice. Let cure 24 hours. Then mix in the rest of the ingredients. We usually add more water. Put in cans and cold pack for three hours.
Yield: 25 qt.
Allen & Ruth Bontrager

HAM LOAF

1 lb. hamburger
1 c. cracker crumbs
1 beaten egg
1/2 lb. wieners, ground
1 tsp. salt
1 tsp. pepper

Glaze:
1/2 c. brown sugar
1/2 c. water
1 T. vinegar
1/2 tsp. mustard

Mix meat as for meatloaf. Put half of the glaze in the meat. Thicken the rest with cornstarch and put on top. Bake one hour at 350º.
Yield:
Virgil & Esther Yoder

MEATLOAF

3 lb. hamburger
2 eggs, beaten
4 c. cracker crumbs (or 1 1/2 c. quick oatmeal)
2 c. milk

1/4 c. fine cut onions (or 1 sm.)
3 tsp. salt
1/2 tsp. pepper

Mix all ingredients together and bake in a rather slow oven, uncovered. When nearly done, add mixture of:
1/2 c. ketchup   1 T. mustard
3 T. brown sugar
Spread on top and bake a little longer.
Raymond & Martha Bontrager   Milo & Ida Bontrager   Wayne & Kathryn Miller

When boiling meat on the bones for broth, let the broth cool several hours or overnight with the bones still in it, which will result in a harder gelled broth. The broth may be reheated to melt it, if necessary, to take out the bones.
Urie & Lizzie Miller

MOCK HAM LOAF

1 lb. hamburger
1 c. cracker crumbs
1 tsp. salt
1/2 glaze mix
Mix together well.
Glaze mix:
1/2 c. brown sugar

1/2 lb. hot dogs ground
1 egg, beaten
Pinch of pepper

1 T. vinegar
1/2 c. hot water

Mix and 1/2 of glaze goes to hamburger mixture. Pour the other half over top of the hamburger mixture. Bake at 350º for 1 hour.
Barbara Miller

TRAIL BOLOGNA

100 lbs. raw meat
2 lbs. tenderquick
24 oz. salt, scant
2 tsp. salt petre
2 lbs. cornstarch
1 1/2 oz. coriander powder

1 tsp. mace
1 tsp. garlic
4 1/2 qt. water
1 c. liquid smoke - if you don't
get your meat smoked

Mix the cut up meat with the tenderquick, salt and salt petre, then grind. Let stand in plastic or stainless steel containers 2-4 days in a cold place. Then grind again and mix the rest of the ingredients. Mix the cornstarch with the water, and add more water if your meat seems too dry and sticky. Cold pack for two hours to can. Note: We often grind twice the first day. Then mix the rest of the ingredients, put into jars and let stand uncovered several days. Then cold pack.
Yield: 50 qt.
Allen & Ruth Bontrager

When canning meat; I like to premix the ground meat with salt, pepper, garlic seasonings to taste. (Test by frying and sampling). Form into patties and fry lightly to keep shape, pack loosely in jars, add water and process. Ready and quick for lunches, especially for families with multiple lunches to pack!

When butchering chicken, I like to leave meat overnight to cool (helps tenderize) with a handful of salt dissolves in water or 2 handfuls if a lot of meat. Next day after breakfast, put a whole chicken in roaster in oven to bake; may add a few veggies if time. Bake covered at 350º. Should be ready by dinner time, cut off meat, salt and season to suit tastebuds.

Disclaimer: We cannot take responsibility for the following home remedies. Use them at your own risk. Always consult your medical doctor before using these remedies.

ARTHRITIS TONIC

Put two tablespoons Knox gelatin, or plain gelatin, in a glass of orange juice. Do not heat. This tastes gritty, but I couldn't believe the results. Fix this mixture and drink at least once a day until you achieve the desired results.

COMFREY SALVE

This works for burns, abrasions, diaper rash, chapped hands, cuts, etc. Harvest about a grocery bag of clean comfrey. With scissors, cut into narrow strips and fill a large pot. Add just enough water to cover comfrey - packing it down well. Simmer on low heat all day, stirring occasionally. Cool overnight and strain off liquid. Add 1 1/2 quarts olive oil or cooking oil to comfrey tea and replace on stove, on medium heat at first to evaporate all the water. This process will take 6-8 hours and must be watched carefully; as you get less water, turn down the heat. Stir more frequently toward the end and don't allow to burn. You will see the fine particles of comfrey clumping together at the bottom, and the bubbling will decrease as you get close to complete evaporation. Add 1-2 ounces of tea tree oil (melaleuca) if you have it. It is a wonderful antiseptic and antifungal. Add 1/2 pound beeswax to thicken the salve, and pour into jelly jars, or any small jar that you can get your fingers into. As it cools it will harden.
Deborah Moore -Midwife

COUGH TEA

(Pneumonia, Asthma, Bronchitis)
In 1 1/2 qt. pan:
1 lemon sliced (washed well)
1 T. honey (or 2)
4 c. water
Bring to a boil, then add:
2 tsp. thyme
2 tsp. plantain
Let steep 10-15 min. Strain. Pour into thermos. Keep hot. Sip 1/2 c. at a time. May use this recipe for whooping cough. Use same first part plus 1 c. flax seed. Simmer 4 hours. If there's less than 1 qt., add water to make 1 qt. Dose: 2 T. four times a day and after coughing spells. Use less for children.
Delilah Stoll

COUGH SYRUPS
Mix a ratio of 1:1 honey and lemon juice and stir well. Store in the refrigerator. It will separate quickly.
Deborah Moore -Midwife

FIRST AID FOR WOUNDS
Pile cayenne pepper on deep wounds to stop the bleeding. Golden Seal powder is very healing on cuts, scrapes and burns. Disinfect with Tea Tree oil first. Put peppermint oil on burns and any open sores.

HEALING SALVE
1 lb. lard   4 tsp. oil of spike
1/2" cube of beeswax   1 tsp. rosin
Melt lard and add wax. Bring to almost boiling then add the rosin. Take outside and add oil of spike (because it smells bad) and cool.
DeVon Miller

HOMEMADE SALVE
1 lb. resin   1 pint linseed oil
1 lb. beeswax   1 lb. fresh lard
Mix all ingredients together and put on the back of your stove. Simmer for three hours, stirring often. This is a very effective salve for any wound.
Menno & Malinda Miller

LUNG FEVER SALVE
1/2 c. unsalted lard   1/2 tsp. camphor

1 tsp. mustard ointment (salve)   1/2 tsp. peppermint oil
1 tsp. turpentine liquid
Grease chest area and put hot water bottle over it. This was Grandma's favorite in her bag of tricks! Yuck! I can still smell it, she used it on me so often just a whiff of it brings back a bushel of memories! But she says it's a sure cure for chest colds. Just make sure you have some on hand always!
Linda (Willis) Bontrager   Delilah Stoll

STOMACH TONIC
Dissolve 1/2 teaspoon dry ginger in a half glass of warm water, or take two ginger capsules with warm water.

JOGGING IN A JUG
5 c. apple juice   1 c. cider vinegar
1 c. grape juice
Take 4 oz. daily for relief of arthritis and to lower blood pressure and cholesterol.
Sam & Ruby Miller

PNEUMONIA SALVE
6 oz. white rosin   4 drams balsam Peru
6 oz. bees wax   4 drams oil turpentine
4 oz. camphor gum   4 drams oil cider
Mix together in an old kettle with 12 oz. lard. Heat until all is melted, then strain into jars and cover, tightly. To use, spread the salve on a cloth, apply to the chest. Cover with a very warm flannel cloth.

WILD CHERRY COUGH SYRUP
Prepare wild cherries as for jelly: sort and clean, add enough water to cover berries and simmer 20-30 minutes. Mash the cherries and let cool enough to check taste after sweetening. Strain off juice. Add honey to sweeten. Reheat for canning process. Pour hot liquid into pint jars, process in hot water bath five minutes. If you have purple coneflower (Echinacea), add 1-2 clean leaves to each jar before filling with syrup.
Deborah Moore -Midwife

WHOOPING COUGH MEDICINE
Take <u>one lemon</u> and slice it thin. Add <u>1/2 pint of flax seed</u> and <u>one quart water</u>. Simmer, but do not boil for four hours. Strain while hot and add <u>two ounces of honey</u>. If there is less than a pint of mixture, add water to make a pint. Dose: One tablespoon four times a day and, in addition, a dose after each severe fit of coughing. This remedy has never been known to fail. A cure being affected in four to five days if given before or when the child first whoops. Will help ease the coughing by allowing the phlegm to be passed out through the stool.

WHITE LINAMENT
1/2 pt. good strong vinegar   1 egg
1/2 pt. turpentine
Shake well. This is a strong liniment!
Sammie & Kathryn Schrock

Happy Birthday!

ALABAMA PECAN PIE

3/4 c. white Karo
5 T. cream
4 eggs
1/4 c. white sugar
1/2 c. brown sugar

1/4 c. melted butter
3/4 c. pecans
1/2 c. fine oatmeal
1 tsp. vanilla

Mix together first five ingredients. Beat well with beater. Add butter, pecans, oatmeal and vanilla. Bake slowly at 300º about 1 hour.
Yield: 1 pie
Ivan & Martha Miller

BUTTER PECAN PIE

6 c. milk
6 T. cornstarch
1 1/2 c. brown sugar
3/4 tsp. salt
1/2 c. milk
3 T. flour
2 egg yolks
2 tsp. vanilla or vanilla butternut flavor
2 T. butter
1/2 c. pecans, lightly chopped
Heat the milk to boiling. Add the next six ingredients to the milk and stir until thick. Add the vanilla flavor and cool. Melt butter until lightly brown and add pecans. Fry on low heat until pecans are lightly browned. When pudding has cooled, add pecans. Pour into two baked pie shells and top with whipped topping.
Yield: 2 pies

BUTTERSCOTCH PIE FILLING

3 c. brown sugar
3 T. butter

10 T. cream

Boil the above together for 5 minutes. Cream together the following and add to the first mixture.

4 c. milk
4 T. flour

2 T. cornstarch
3 eggs, beaten

Cook until thickened. Top with whipped cream. This pie we thought was so good. Barbara and I would sneak it upstairs under our bed. M-M-M!!
Yield: 2 pies
Linda (Willis) Bontrager

CHOCOLATE PUDDING PIE FILLING

Heat:

2 c. milk   1/3 c. sugar

Mix:

3/4 c. sugar   2 T. Nestle quick cocoa

3 T. cornstarch   1 egg yolk

When cooked, take off heat and add vanilla, pinch of salt and a chunk of butter. Pour into baked pie crust. When cooled, put your favorite whipped topping on and serve.

Yield: 1 pie

Wayne & Kathryn Miller

CRISCO PIE CRUST CRUMBS

1 - 3 lb. can Crisco   1 1/2 T. salt

5 lb. flour

Mix until all crumbly. Store in fix and mix; add a little water when ready to use. One big handful of crumbs is usually enough for one single pie crust. This is handy to keep on hand. Makes baking go faster.

Linda (Willis) Bontrager

GRANDMA EMMA'S PIE CRUST

1 heaping cup flour   Pinch of salt

1 spoonful lard

Mix together until crumbly, then add enough water until right consistency. When I was young, I always thought pie to be a very special thing. No one in our family knew how to make it, so we never had any. One summer when I spent a few days by Grandma and Grandpa, I pestered Grandma to teach me how to make a pie. So finally, Grandma went to work and rolled out all the mysteries of pie dough for me! Oh how wonderful my new-found knowledge was to me. So pie has always held special memories for me.

Linda (Willis) Bontrager

LEMON SPONGE PIE

Juice and rind of one lemon or   3 eggs, separated

1/4 c. lemon juice   1/2 tsp. salt

1 c. sugar   2 T. butter

3 level T. flour   1 1/2 c. hot milk

Cream butter; add sugar and egg yolks. Beat well. Add flour, salt, lemon juice, grated rind and milk. Fold in stiffly beaten egg whites. Pour in unbaked pie shell. Bake at 350º for 40-45 minutes.

Yield: 1 pie

MOLASSES NUT PIE

2 eggs, well beaten
1 c. white Karo
1/3 c. white sugar
2 T. melted butter

2 T. flour
1 tsp. vanilla
1/4 tsp. salt
1 c. nuts

Mix all ingredients together. Pour into unbaked pie shell. Sprinkle one c. ground nuts on top. Bake at 350º for 45 minutes.
Yield: 1 - 8 pie
Amos & Elizabeth Miller

NO BAKE CREAM PIE

1/4 c. cornstarch
1/2 c. white sugar
1/2 c. brown sugar
1 egg, beaten

1 tsp. vanilla
Pinch of salt
1 stick butter

Put 2 c. milk in saucepan and bring to a boil. Mix together egg, sugar, cornstarch, salt and the rest of the milk into hot milk. Cook until thickened. Add vanilla and butter. Cool and pour into baked pie shell. Sprinkle with nutmeg. Delicious! Tastes similar to cream pie.
Linda (Willis) Bontrager

PEACH CUSTARD PIE

1 c. sugar
2 T. flour
1/8 tsp. salt
1 egg, beaten
2 T. butter, melted

1 tsp. vanilla
1 c. milk
2 c. fresh peaches, finely cut
Cinnamon

Mix the dry ingredients together. Combine with the beat egg, vanilla, milk, peaches and butter. Pour into an unbaked pie shell. Sprinkle the top with cinnamon. Bake in a moderate oven until the center is almost set.
Yield: 1 lg. pie
Urie & Lizzie Ann Miller

PEANUT BUTTER PIE

1 c. Karo
1/2 c. sugar
1/3 c. peanut butter

3 eggs, beaten
1/2 tsp. vanilla
1/2 c. oatmeal or coconut

Mix ingredients together and pour into one unbaked pie shell and bake.
Sammie & Kathryn Schrock

PEANUT BUTTER CUP PIE

1 1/2 c. white sugar
3 T. flour
3 T. cocoa

3/4 c. milk
3 beaten eggs
1 1/2 tsp. vanilla

Combine these ingredients and pour in 2 unbaked pie shells. Bake at 350º for 30 min. or until set. Cool. Topping:

8 oz. cream cheese
1 c. powdered sugar
1/2 c. peanut butter

2 c. whipped topping
1 tsp. vanilla

Combine ingredients and pour in 2 chilled chocolate filled pies. Put topping on top and sprinkle with shredded chocolate.
Yield: 16 servings
Irene Miller

PECAN PIE

3 eggs, beaten
1 c. light Karo
1 c. sugar (half brown and half white)

2 T. melted butter
1 tsp. vanilla
1 c. pecans

Pour in unbaked pie shell. Bake at 400º for 10 min., then at 325º until set. I like to take a sheet cake pan and line it with pie dough. Then doubling this recipe is just right for that size pan. This works great to take along to ice cream suppers, etc. cut in squares.
Linda (Willis) Bontrager   Raymond & Martha Bontrager

PIE CRUST

2 c. lard or shortening
6 c. flour
3 tsp. baking powder

1 egg
Water
Salt

Break the egg into a measuring cup. Fill with water to make one cup. Add the rest of the ingredients and mix well. If lard is soft, use cold water.
Yield: 6 - two-crust pies
Sammie & Kathryn Schrock

PUMPKIN CHIFFON PIE

1/4 c. milk
1 pkg. Knox gelatin
3 egg yolks - set whites aside
1 c. sugar
1 T. flour

1/2 tsp. salt
1/4 tsp. ginger
1 tsp. cinnamon
1 c. strained pumpkin

Dissolve gelatin in the milk. Mix the rest of the ingredients together and bring to a boil and keep stirring. Now mix in the gelatin mixture, while hot. Cool, then beat egg whites and fold in. Pour into baked pie shell and sprinkle nutmeg on top. Place in refrigerator, serve with whipped cream.
Yield: 1 large pie
Milo & Ida Bontrager

PUMPKIN PIE

2 c. pumpkin or butternut squash
2 c. sugar
2 T. flour (rounded)
2 eggs, beaten
1/2 tsp. cinnamon

1/2 tsp. nutmeg
1/2 tsp. allspice
1 tsp. salt
1 qt. milk

Mix all together and pour into two unbaked pie shells. Bake at 350º for one hour or until middle is set.
Yield: 2 pies
Oba & Laura Borkholder

RAISIN TART PIE

1 c. corn syrup
1 c. raisins
1/4 c. melted butter
3 eggs, yolks beaten

Pinch of salt
1/2 c. sugar
1/4 c. water
1 tsp. vanilla

Mix all ingredients together. Line muffin tins with pie dough and pour the mixture into the pans. Bake at 350º After they're done, beat the two egg whites until stiff and put them on top of the pies. Place them back in the oven until lightly brown.
Yield: 10-12 tart-sized pies
Alva & Katie Ann Bontrager

RHUBARB CREAM PIE

1 1/4 c. sugar
2 T. flour, rounded
1/4 tsp. salt

3/4 c. cream
2 egg yolks
1 1/2 c. rhubarb, cut fine

Beat together the cream and egg yolks. Stir in sugar, flour, salt, and then add the rhubarb. Bake in a slow oven - 325º. Apples or peaches can also be used. Pineapple and coconut together make a great combination.
Yield: 1 pie
David & Mary Kauffman

RHUBARB PIE

1 1/2 c. rhubarb
1 1/4 c. sugar
2 egg yolks, beaten
2 T. flour

1 c. cream
1 tsp. vanilla
2 beaten egg whites

Put rhubarb in unbaked pie crust. Mix the rest together and add beaten egg whites last. Bake at 425º for 10 min., and then reduce to 325º and bake until set.
Linda (Willis) Bontrager

146

STRAWBERRY GLAZE
3 c. water   3/4 c. clear jell
1 1/4 c. white sugar   4 1/2 oz. strawberry Jello
Bring water and sugar to a boil. Add thickening made of clear jell with enough water added to make a paste. Remove from heat and add Jello. Cool and add desired amount of strawberries.
Yield: 2 pies

THREE WALNUT PIE
1 1/2 c. sugar   5 c. milk
5 T. flour   1 c. white Karo
Pinch of salt
6 eggs (whites can be beaten and added last, if desired)
Make pie dough the same as you would for any other pie. Mix the sugar, flour and salt together. Mix the remaining ingredients together thoroughly. Add one c. chopped walnuts in each unbaked pie shell. Now measure liquid by cups to each pie. Start baking at 400º for 20 minutes. Slowly reduce heat to 300º when pie has baked one hour.
Yield:
Grandma Emma Miller

VELVET CUSTARD PIE
4 eggs   1 tsp. vanilla
1 c. sugar   Pinch of salt
2 1/2 c. scalded milk
Beat eggs, sugar, vanilla and salt together. Heat milk until scalding, then pour into rest of ingredients. Pour into unbaked pie shell and sprinkle nutmeg on top. Bake at 425º for 10 min. Reduce heat to 325º until done. Do not let custard pie bubble or "cook." It makes a big difference in taste. If it doesn't cook, it has a velvety texture.
Linda (Willis) Bontrager   Raymond & Martha Bontrager

WONDER CRUNCH PIE
3 eggs   1 c. lukewarm water
3/4 c. sugar   1 tsp. vanilla
2 tsp. melted butter   1/2 c. Grapenuts
1 c. white Karo   1/2 c. walnuts, optional
Beat the three eggs well. Add the next five ingredients. Stir in the grapenuts. Pour the mixture into an unbaked pie shell and bake at 375º. A pie baker can soon tell when the pie is done. It will puff up similar to a custard pie.
Yield: 1 pie
Alva & Katie Ann Bontrager

BROCCOLI SALAD

1 bundle broccoli, cut small
1/2 c. onion, diced
1/2 lb. bacon, fried crisp and crumbled
1 med. head cauliflower, cut small

1/2 c. salted sunflower seeds
1/2 c. raisins (optional)
2 c. diced fresh tomato
2 c. grated cheddar cheese
1 sm. onion, chopped

Dressing:
1/2 c. white sugar
3/4 c. sour cream
3/4 c. or less salad dressing

2 T. vinegar (optional)
1/2 tsp. salt (optional)
Hidden Valley Ranch dressing mix

Mix first six ingredients together, then just before serving, mix in the next three.
Yield:
Virgil & Esther Yoder   Joni & Emma Sue Miller
Linda (Willis) Bontrager

CINNAMON APPLESAUCE SALAD

1/2 c. red hots (candy)
2 c. boiling water

1 - 6 oz. box cherry Jello
2 c. thick applesauce

Mix red hots and boiling water. Heat until red hots are dissolved, then add Jello and stir until Jello is dissolved. Add applesauce and mix well. Pour into a ring mold (if desired) and chill until firm. Eat with cottage cheese.
Yield:
Virgil & Esther Yoder

COLE SLAW

1 lg. head cabbage, shredded
1 onion, chopped fine
1 green pepper, diced
1 c. celery, diced
2 c. sugar

1/2 tsp. salt
1/2 c. white vinegar
1/4 c. water
1 tsp. celery seed if desired
1 tsp. mustard seed if desired

Mix all together and store in the refrigerator for a few hours. It can be made ahead and frozen for a few days and served while still a little icy.
Joni & Emma Sue Miller

GRAPE SALAD

8 oz. cream cheese
1/2 c. powdered sugar
8 oz. sour cream

8 oz. Cool Whip
4 lb. seedless grapes

Mix together first four ingredients. Add grapes, whole.
Ella E. Miller

COTTAGE CHEESE SALAD

1 c. milk
1 lg. pkg. marshmallows
1 pkg. cream cheese
1/2 c. sugar

1 T. plain gelatin
1 pkg. Dream Whip
1 can crushed pineapple
2 lbs. cottage cheese

Melt the milk, marshmallows and cream cheese in a double boiler. Soak the gelatin and sugar in a little water until it is dissolved. Add to the hot mixture. Mix all ingredients together and let set.
Herman & Carolina Miller

LETTUCE SLAW SALAD

Lettuce, snipped
Cabbage, shredded
Cheddar cheese, shredded
1 c. salad dressing

1/2 c. sugar
2 T. mustard
1/2 tsp. salt

Place a layer of lettuce in the bottom of a glass cake pan, then add a layer of cabbage. Beat together the last four ingredients and drizzle over the cabbage. Top with the cheddar cheese.
Yield:
David & Mary Kauffman

MARSHMALLOW CHEESE SALAD

1 lb. marshmallows
1/2 c. milk
1 pt. creamed cottage cheese
1 - 8 oz. pkg. cream cheese

1 can crushed pineapple
1 c. chopped nuts
1 c. whipping cream

Melt marshmallows in milk in the top of a double boiler. Cream the two cheeses. Add the melted marshmallows, slightly cooled. When the mixture is no longer warm, add drained pineapple and nuts. Fold in whipped cream. Chill. Variation: Maraschino cherries may be used instead of nuts.
Menno & Malinda Miller

POTATO SALAD

12 c. potatoes, cooked & shredded
12 eggs
    Dressing:
3 c. salad dressing
3 T. mustard
2 c. sugar

1/2 c. onion
1 1/2 c. celery

1/2 c. milk
4 tsp. salt
3 T. vinegar

Cook potatoes until soft. Put through salad maker (also the hard-boiled eggs). Mix well and refrigerate overnight or several hours before serving. One and a half batches fills a Fix-N-Mix bowl.
Yield: Approx. 1 gal.
Urie & Lizzie Ann Miller   Aaron & Irene Miller

SALAMI

2 - 2 1/2 lb. good ground beef
1/2 tsp. onion powder
1/2 tsp. garlic powder
2 T. curing salt (Tender-Quick)

1 T. mustard seed
1 1/2 tsp. liquid smoke
Pinch of crushed red pepper
3/4 c. water

Mix all ingredients together. Shape into 3 rolls on foil and wrap. Refrigerate for 24 hours. Open up foil and bake at 300º for 1 hour and 15 minutes.

SLOPPY JOE BARBECUE (FOR SANDWICHES)

10 lbs. hamburger
5 c. onions, chopped
1 c. chopped celery
1/4 c. salt mixed with
1 1/4 T. pepper
1 c. vinegar

3/4 c. prepared mustard
1 1/2 c. brown sugar
2/3 c. Worcestershire sauce
5 c. ketchup
4 c. beef broth

Brown the hamburger and onion with flour as it will thicken somewhat with the other ingredients added. Steam for 10 minutes. Pack hot into jars and seal process for two hours in a hot water bath.
Yield: Approx. 9 qt.

TACO SALAD

1 head lettuce
1 can kidney beans - drained
1 lb. ground beef, browned and seasoned with taco seasoning
2 medium tomatoes, diced
1 medium onion
5 oz. cheese, grated
1 pkg. nacho chips or Doritos

1/4 c. vinegar
1/3 c. salad oil
1/3 c. ketchup
1/2 c. sugar
1 medium onion
1 T. Worcestershire sauce
Pinch of salt
Dash of pepper

Put everything from vinegar on down in a jar and shake. Layer first six ingredients in given order. Add crushed chips and dressing just before serving.
Yield: 10 servings
Amos & Elizabeth Miller

In every blossom,
   that is tucked away.
For some one who is sick,
   A friendly thought
      is sent your way,
And special wishes..
Hope you're soon well
      to stay!.....

BROCCOLI SOUP

1 head broccoli   1 onion, chopped
1-2 c. turkey bacon or turkey ham   1 sm. can cream of mushroom soup

Cook broccoli, not more than five minutes, and let set with lid on a few minutes. Add the other ingredients and heat slowly. Do not boil. You may add milk to suit your family. Delicious!
Yield: 8 or more servings
Monroe & Elsie Miller

BROCCOLI CHEESE SOUP

3/4 c. onions, chopped   2 pkg. (10 oz.) broccoli, chopped
6 c. water   1/4 tsp. garlic salt
6 chicken bouillon cubes   6 c. milk
8 oz. fine noodles   1 lb. Velveeta cheese
Salt

Saute the onions for 3 minutes in oil or margarine. Add this to the water and bouillon cubes. Stir well until cubes dissolve. Bring to a boil and add the noodles and salt. Stir in broccoli and garlic salt. Cook for 4 minutes and add the milk and Velveeta cheese. Stir until melted.
Jacob & Loretta Shetler

CHICKEN NOODLE SOUP

1 bunch celery   carrots, optional
1 lb. noodles   parsley, optional
2 qt. diced potatoes   3 chickens
6 medium onions

Cook each separately until almost done. Remove cooked chicken from bones. Bring broth to a boil and add noodles. Remove from heat and add the rest of the ingredients. Season with salt and pepper. Add fried chicken seasoning, Season All, or chicken base. Cold pack for three hours or ten lb. pressure for 3/4 hour. Dilute when opening with milk or water.
Yield: 12 qt.

OLD FASHIONED CREAM OF TOMATO SOUP

1 qt. tomato juice   2 T. sugar
1 qt. canned tomato chunks or juice   1/2 c. chopped onion
1 c. chicken broth or cream of   1/8 tsp. baking soda
   chicken   1 1/2 c. heavy cream
1/4 c. butter   3/4 c. flour

In a saucepan, combine the first 6 ingredients. Cover and let simmer; add baking soda. Blend cream and flour and pour into boiling mixture. Thickness depends on if you use cream of chicken, etc. Adjust however you like it. This is one of our favorites.
Linda (Willis) Bontrager

CHILI SOUP

2 qt. tomato juice
2 qt. water
1/2 c. brown sugar
2 T. onion salt
3 T. chili powder
1 c. lentils

1 qt. kidney (or other) beans
Dash of sorghum
1 lb. hamburger, browned with onions
1 lg. onion

Combine juice, water, brown sugar, onion salt and chili powder in a kettle. Fry the hamburger and onion until brown and add to the kettle. Bring to the boiling point and add lentils and sorghum. It's best if simmered slowly several hours and stirred occasionally. Note: This recipe calls for salutes tomato juice or else soup will be too salty.
Yield: 6 qt.
Monroe & Elsie Miller   Urie & Lizzie Ann Miller

CHUNKY BEEF SOUP

1 lb. smoked bacon, fried and crumbled (optional)
8 lbs. hamburger, fried and crumbled
2 lg. onions, chopped and browned with hamburger
2 qt. navy beans
2 qt. diced carrots
4 qt. diced potatoes
2 qt. peas

2 qt. whole kernel corn
1-2 qt. diced celery
4 qt. tomato juice
4-6 qt. beef broth
2 1/2 gals. water
5 c. Perma Flo
1/3 c. salt
1 c. sugar
1 - 2 T. chili powder, if desired

Boil vegetables, separately, but not too soft. Bring broth and most of the water to a boil and thicken with Perma Flo, which has been mixed with some water. Bring to a boil again, then mix everything together. Ladle into jars, but do not fill quite up to the neck. Process in a hot water bath for two hours. Let jars set in water a bit after turning off burner to keep soup from bubbling out from underneath lids.
Yield: Approx. 27 qt.
Urie & Lizzie Ann Miller

POTATOES & HAM SOUP

1 lg. onion sautéed in 3/4 lb. butter. Add enough flour to make a thick paste. Add 5 qt. milk and five qt. shredded potatoes that have been cooked in enough water to cover potatoes. Add 5-6 lbs. chopped ham. Add a 2 lb. box of Velveeta and season with salt and Lawry's salt.
Yield: 5 gal.
Jacob & Loretta Shetler

TOMATO WEINER SOUP

16 qt. kettle of tomato juice
5 ribs celery
7 onions
2 1/2 c. flour
2 1/2 c. sugar
5 T. salt
6 T. parsley flakes
1 T. of garlic
1 T. onion salt
1 T. celery salt
2 cans evaporated milk
1 lb. butter

Put the onions and celery through the grinder and cook until soft. Add these to the tomato juice. Make a sauce with the remaining ingredients. Pour the sauce into the hot juice mixture to thicken and bring to a boil. Add the butter last. Cut two hotdogs into each qt. jar (more or less to taste), then fill jars with soup. Pressure cook for ten minutes at ten lb. of pressure.
Yield: Approx. 18 qt.
Oba & Laura Borkholder

SCALLOPED CAULIFLOWER

1 lg. head cauliflower
3 hard boiled eggs
2 c. med. white sauce.
1/2 tsp. salt
1/4 tsp. pepper
1 c. buttered bread crumbs
1/4 c. grated cheese

Break cauliflower into pieces and cook in salt water until tender. Drain and place the layers of the cauliflower, diced egg and white sauce in a greased casserole. Put a layer of buttered crumbs and cheese over the top. Bake at 375º for 25 minutes.
Herman & Carolina Miller

SPLIT PEA SOUP

1 lb. split peas
3 qt. water
1 sm. ham shank
1 lg. chopped onion
2 T. chicken bouillon
1/2 tsp. garlic powder
1/2 tsp. oregano leaves
1/4-1/2 tsp. pepper
1 bay leaf
1 1/2 c. thinly sliced carrots
1 c. chopped celery

Simmer for 1 1/2 hours. Stir in carrots and celery, simmer uncovered again for 2 - 2 1/2 hours until soup reaches desired thickness.
Wilma M. Miller

ZUCCHINI FRITTERS

1 c. grated zucchini
1 shredded carrot
2 T. minced onion
1/2 c. flour
1/4 tsp. Lawry's salt
1/2 tsp. garlic salt
1/8 tsp. salt
1/8 tsp. pepper

Mix and let set a little before frying. Good!
Menno & Malinda Miller

May your Birthday
be a very special day,
Beginning a brand
New year and
Happy all year..

Good Luck

CORNSTARCH

1 qt. milk
1 egg yolk
2 T. cornstarch, heaping
1/4 c. white sugar

1/4 tsp. salt
3/4 c. brown sugar (or to taste)
Vanilla

Heat the milk. Mix the cornstarch and yolk with the white sugar. Stir in a little cold milk. Stir this mixture into heated (boiling point) milk. Stir until thick. Remove from the stove. Add salt, vanilla and brown sugar. Eat warm with French toast or fried potatoes, green beans, sausage and eggs, or even graham cracker bits. Use leftovers for a pudding. Great for a supper dish.
Yield: 4-6 servings
Allen & Ruth Bontrager

NOODLES

2 c. egg yolks (2 dz.)
1 1/2 c. boiling water

Flour

Beat the egg yolks and boiling water together until foamy. Put a fix and mix bowl on a kitchen scale and put enough flour in to measure four lbs. Pour the egg mixture over the flour and stir together with a large fork. Place a lid on it and let set for 10 minutes. Then work it together and put through a cutter. No flour mess.
Yield: 2 batches = 1 - 50 lb. lard can of noodles.
Sammie & Kathryn Schrock

ROYAL BAKING POWDER

2 T. cream of tartar
1 T. cornstarch

1 T. baking soda

Measure carefully and sift together. It is important to sift and mix well. Store in an airtight container.
Ivan & Martha Miller

S'MORES

Marshmallows
Graham wafers

Chocolate candy bars

Roast marshmallows over campfire. Sandwich between two graham wafers and a small square of chocolate.
Menno & Malinda Miller

INDEX

159

COOKING FOR A CROWD

Food Quantities for Serving 25 People

Sandwich/Soup-Type Meals:
Bread = 50 slices or 3 (1-lb.) loaves
Butter = 1/2 lb.
Jams and preserves = 1 1/2 lb.
Mayonnaise = 1 c.
Mixed filling, meat, eggs, fish - 1 1/2 qts.
Mixed filling, sweet/fruit = 1 qt.
Lettuce - 1 1/2 heads
Rolls = 4 doz.
Crackers = 1 1/2 lb.
Cheese, 2 oz. per serving = 3 lb.
Soup = 1 1/2 gal.
Salad dressings = 1 pt.
Meat, Poultry, or Fish:
Hot dogs, beef = 6 1/2 lbs.
Hamburger = 9 lbs.
Turkey or chicken = 13 lbs.
Fish, lg. whole, round = 13 lbs.
Fish fillets or steak = 7 1/2 lbs.
Salads, Casseroles, Vegetables:
Potato salad = 4 1/4 qts.
Scalloped Potatoes = 4 1/2 qts. Or 1-12x20 pan
Mashed potatoes = 9 lb.
Canned vegetables = 1-#10 can
Spaghetti = 1 1/4 gal.
Baked beans = 3/4 gal.
Jello salad = 3/4 gal.
Fresh Vegetables:
Carrots, 3 oz. or 1/2 c. = 6 - 1 lb.
Tomatoes = 3-5 lb.
Ice Cream:
Brick = 3 1/4 qts.
Bulk = 2 1/4 qts.
Beverages:
Coffee = 1/2 lb. and 1 1/2 gal. Water
Tea = 1/12 lb. and 1 1/2 gal. Water
Lemonade = 10-15 lemons, 1 1/2 gal. water
Desserts:
Watermelon = 37 1/2 lbs.
Cake = 1-10x12 sheet cake, or 2-8" layer cakes
Fruit cup, 1/2 c. per serving = 3 qt.
Whipping cream = 1 pt.

Food Quantities for Serving 50 People

Sandwich/Soup-Type Meals:
Bread = 100 slices or 6 (1-lb.) loaves
Butter = 3/4 to1 lb.
Jams and preserves = 3 lb.
Mayonnaise = 2 to 3 c.
Mixed filling, meat, eggs, fish = 2 1/2 to 3 qts.
Mixed filling, sweet/fruit = 1 3/4 to 2 qts.
Lettuce = 2 1/2 to 3 heads
Rolls = 8 doz.
Crackers = 3 lb.
Cheese, 2 oz. per serving = 6 lb.
Soup = 3 gal.
Salad dressings = 2 1/2 pt.
Meat, Poultry, or Fish:
Hot dogs, beef = 13 lbs.
Hamburger = 18 lbs.
Turkey or chicken = 25 to 35 lbs.
Fish, large whole, round = 25 lbs.
Fish fillets or steak = 15 lbs.
Salads, Casseroles, Vegetables:
Potato salad = 1 1/4 gal.
Scalloped potatoes = 8 1/2 qts.

Mashed potatoes = 18-20 lb.
Canned vegetables = 2 1/2 #10 cans
Spaghetti = 2 1/2 gal.
Baked beans = 1 1/4 gal.
Jello salad = 1 1/4 gal.
Fresh Vegetables:
Carrots, 3 oz. or 1/2 c. = 12 1/2 lb.
Tomatoes = 7-10 lb.
Ice Cream:
Brick = 6 1/2 qts.
Bulk = 4 1/2 qts or 1 1/4 gal.
Beverages:
Coffee = 1 lb. and 3 gal. water
Tea = 1/6 lb. and 3 gal. water
Lemonade = 20 to 30 lemons and 3 gal. water
Desserts:
Watermelon = 75 lbs.
Cake = 1-12x20 sheet cake or 3-10" layer cakes
Fruit cup, 1/2 c. per serving = 6 qt.
Whipping cream = 1 qt.

Food Quantities for Serving 100 People

Sandwich/Soup-Type Meals:
Bread = 200 slices or 12 (1-lb.) loaves
Butter = 1 1/2 lbs.
Jams and preserves = 6 lb.
Mayonnaise = 4 to 6 c.
Mixed filling, meat, eggs, fish = 5 to 6 qts.
Mixed filling, sweet/fruit = 2 1/2 to 4 qts.
Lettuce = 5 to 6 heads
Rolls = 16 doz.
Crackers = 6 lb.
Cheese, 2 oz. per serving = 12 lb.
Soup = 6 gal.
Salad dressings = 1/2 gal.
Meat, Poultry, or Fish:
Hot dogs, beef = 25 lbs.
Hamburger = 35 lbs.
Turkey or chicken = 50 to 75 lbs.
Fish, large whole, round = 50 lbs.
Fish fillets or steak = 30 lbs.
Salads, Casseroles, Vegetables:
Potato Salad = 4 1/4 gal.
Scalloped potatoes = 17 qts.
Mashed potatoes = 25-35 lb.
Canned vegetables = 4 #10 cans
Spaghetti = 5 gal.
Baked beans = 2 1/2 gal.
Jello salad = 2 1/2 gal.
Fresh Vegetables:
Carrots, 3 oz. or 1/2 c. = 25 lb.
Tomatoes = 14-20 lb.
Ice Cream:
Brick = 12 1/2 qts
Bulk = 9 qts. Or 2 1/2 gal.
Beverages:
Coffee = 2 lbs. and 6 gal. water
Tea = 1/3 lb. and 6 gal. water
Lemonade = 40 to 60 lemons and 6 gal. water
Desserts:
Watermelon = 150 lbs.
Cake = 2-12x20 sheet cakes or 6-10" layer cakes
Fruit cup, 1/2 c. per serving = 12 qt.
Whipping cream = 2 qts.

GIVE A GIFT THAT WILL BE APPRECIATED ALL YEAR!
MILLER FAMILY COOKBOOK

To get additional copies of this cookbook, send check or money order to: Abana Books 6523 TR 346 Millersburg, OH 44654

Shipping and handling is $3 for the first copy. Add $1 for each copy thereafter to the same address.

Qty   Total

$9.95 X _____ = _____

FREE Bonus
Receive 26 mouth watering ice cream, sherbert and frozen yogurt recipes with purchase of a cookbook.

Shipping & Handling = _____

Total = _____

My Name _____

My Address _____

My City/State/Zip _____

❑ Please send me information on how I can retail this book at my place of business.

❑ Please send me information on how I can use this book as a fundraiser for my church or school.

--------------------------✂--

GET ADDITIONAL COPIES!
MILLER FAMILY COOKBOOK

To get additional copies of this cookbook, send check or money order to: Abana Books 6523 TR 346 Millersburg, OH 44654

Shipping and handling is $3 for the first copy. Add $1 for each copy thereafter to the same address.

Qty   Total

$9.95 X _____ = _____

FREE Bonus
Receive 26 mouth watering ice cream, sherbert and frozen yogurt recipes with purchase of a cookbook.

Shipping & Handling = _____

Total = _____

My Name _____

My Address _____

My City/State/Zip _____

❑ Please send me information on how I can retail this book at my place of business.

❑ Please send me information on how I can use this book as a fundraiser for my church or school.

Life of Emma Miller

Grandma of the Miller Family. *"At this time (1999) I am 98 and have 76 grandchildren, 382 great-grandchildren and 46 great-great-grandchildren."* An autobiography of Emma Miller (Levi Miller Family) born in 1901. Take a trip down memory lane with her as she recounts how her Amish life was like growing up in Colorado, Indiana, and Michigan in the days of cowboys, log cabins, the Great Depression, WW II, and when eggs were 12¢ a dozen. From near scrapes with death to the humorous, make sure you have plenty of time when you begin reading it. Also included is Life in Colorado. $4.95 + $2 Shipping

Send a check or money order (US funds) to:
ABANA   BOOKS
6523 TR 346
Millersburg, OH 44654

-------------✂--

LIFE   OF   EMMA   MILLER

Shipping and handling is $2 for the first copy. Add $ .50 for each copy thereafter.

Price	Qty	Total
$4.95 X _____	=	_____
Shipping & Handling = _____		

Total ...._____

Send To:

Name _____

Address _____

City/State/Zip _____

Telephone _____

FUNDRAISING SUCCESS!

You collect the recipes and we do the rest. Let us show you how easy it is to create your own cookbook . . . *or use our cookbook for raising immediate funds.*

Features will include:

Professional Typesetting

Information about your organization

Alphabetized Table of Contents and Index

Colorful full length spiral bindings to enable your book to lie flat

Coupon Page to help you sell your cookbooks

Enrollment in an Advantage selling program with the world's largest
bookstore boasting over a million customers and others like it!

---------------✂--

Fundraising Success Request

Yes, Please rush me FREE information on how we can use your fundraising plan. We would like to use . . .

❏ . . . our own cookbook.

❏ . . . your cookbook for immediate sales.

Organization _____

Name _____

Address _____

City/State/Zip _____

Home PH _____ Work PH _____

Send your request to Abana Books